NEW MERMAIDS

OSCAR WILDE

LADY WINDERMERE'S FAN

edited by Ian Small

Professor of English Literature
University of Birmingham

A & C Black • London
WW Norton • New York

Second edition 1999
Reprinted with new cover 2002
A & C Black Publishers Limited
37 Soho Square
London W1D 3QZ
www.acblack.com

ISBN 0-7136-6667-6

Published in the United States of America
by W. W. Norton & Company Inc.
500 Fifth Avenue, New York, NY 10110

ISBN 0-393-90048-7

CIP catalogue records for this book are available
from the British Library and the Library of Congress.

Printed in Great Britain by
Bookmarque Ltd, Croydon, Surrey

NEW MERMAIDS

General editor: Brian Gibbons
Professor of English Literature, University of Münster

Reconstruction of an early twentieth-century
proscenium stage by C. Walter Hodges

CONTENTS

ACKNOWLEDGEMENTS

I am grateful to Mr Merlin Holland for permission to consult and reproduce copyright material and to the following institutions for making available material in their possession: the British Library; the Harry Ransom Research Center, the University of Texas at Austin; the William Andrews Clark Memorial Library, the University of California at Los Angeles; the Library of Trinity College, Dublin. I am also grateful to the staff of the Inter-Library Loans Department at Birmingham University.

Friends and colleagues have been helpful to me in preparing the annotation. I would like to record my gratitude to James Boulton, Ralph Davies, Tom Davis, Ramon Drewek, Ian Ross and Janet Small. John Stokes and Russell Jackson have given freely of their time and of their expert knowledge of the theatre of the time: I am greatly indebted to both. I am grateful also for the invaluable suggestions and corrections made by Charles Allen and Brian Gibbons.

Birmingham, March 1980   I.S.

NOTE TO THE 1999 REVISED EDITION

This revision differs from my original 1980 edition of *Lady Windermere's Fan* in the following respects: the sections entitled 'The Play', 'The Play and its Drafts', the 'Note on the Text and Textual and Critical Annotation' and the 'Note on Staging' have been brought up to date by taking account of developments in recent critical and scholarly writing on Wilde. The biographical account of Wilde (by Russell Jackson), the text of the play, and the textual and critical apparatus remain unchanged, save for the silent correction of errors. I have taken the opportunity of a revised edition to extend and bring up to date the section on 'Further Reading'. I am grateful to Josephine Guy, who read through the revised introductory material and made valuable comments.

Birmingham, March 1999   I.S.

ABBREVIATIONS

References to *Lady Windermere's Fan* are to the line numbers of the present edition. Other works by Wilde (except *The Importance of Being Earnest*) are referred to by the title of the volume in which they appear in Robert Ross's edition of the *Works* (14 vols., 1908). Reference to *The Importance of Being Earnest* is to the edition by Russell Jackson in the New Mermaid series. I have given additional references to the page numbers of the Collins's *Complete Works* (1967), designated *CW*. *The Letters of Oscar Wilde*, ed. R. Hart-Davis (1962; revised edn., 1963) is abbreviated to *Letters*.

The drafts and texts of *Lady Windermere's Fan* referred to in the edition are as follows:

BL	First manuscript draft under the title of 'Lady Windermere's Fan' at the British Library (BL Add MS 37943).
Cms	Manuscript entitled 'Lady Windermere's Fan' at the William Andrews Clark Memorial Library (Finzi 2460).
C1	Typescript entitled 'A Good Woman' at the William Andrews Clark Memorial Library (Finzi 2448).
C2	Typescript entitled 'Lady Windermere's Fan' at the William Andrews Clark Memorial Library (Finzi 2459).
T	Typescript entitled 'A Good Woman' at the Harry Ransom Humanities Research Center, University of Texas at Austin.
LC	Licensing Copy, British Library (dated 15 February 1892) (BL Add MS 53492).
F	*Lady Windermere's Fan* by Oscar Wilde (London: Samuel French Ltd., n.d.).
1st ed.	*Lady Windermere's Fan* by Oscar Wilde (London: Elkin Mathews and John Lane, 1893).

Other Abbreviations

Manners and Rules	*Manners and Rules of Good Society* by A Member of the Aristocracy (1888).
Habits	*The Habits of Good Society: A Handbook of Etiquette* (1890).
OED	*Oxford English Dictionary*.

In the notes the names of characters are abbreviated to initials. So, for example, Lady Windermere is Lady W., and the Duchess of Berwick is the Duchess of B.

s.d	stage direction
R.	Right
L.	Left
C.	Centre
R.C.	Right of Centre
L.C.	Left of Centre
R.U.E.	Right Upper Entrance
L.U.E.	Left Upper Entrance

INTRODUCTION

The Author

André Gide describes Oscar Wilde as he appeared in 1891, when 'his success was so certain that it seemed that it preceded [him] and that all he needed to do was go forward and meet it':

> ... He was rich; he was tall; he was handsome; laden with good fortune and honours. Some compared him to an Asiatic Bacchus; others to some Roman emperor; others to Apollo himself – and the fact is that he was radiant.[1]

The melodramatic contrast between this triumphant figure and the pathetic convict serving two years' hard labour was drawn by Wilde himself in *De Profundis*, the letter written from prison to his lover, Lord Alfred Douglas. He described his transfer in November 1895 from Wandsworth to Reading Gaol, little care being taken for his privacy:

> From two o'clock till half-past two on that day I had to stand on the centre platform at Clapham Junction in convict dress and handcuffed, for the world to look at. I had been taken out of the Hospital Ward without a moment's notice being given to me. Of all possible objects I was the most grotesque. When people saw me they laughed. Each train as it came up swelled the audience. Nothing could exceed their amusement. That was of course before they knew who I was. As soon as they had been informed, they laughed still more. For half an hour I stood there in the grey November rain surrounded by a jeering mob.[2]

Wilde insisted that his life was as much an artistic endeavour as his works – in *De Profundis* he claimed to have been 'a man who stood

---

[1] André Gide, 'In Memoriam' from *Oscar Wilde*, translated Bernard Frechtman (New York, 1949); quoted from the extract in Richard Ellmann, ed., *Oscar Wilde: A Collection of Critical Essays* (Englewood Cliffs, N.J., 1969), 25–34. The principal sources for the present account of Wilde's career are H. Montgomery Hyde, *Oscar Wilde* (1975), Richard Ellmann, *Oscar Wilde* (1987), and Rupert Hart-Davis, ed., *The Letters of Oscar Wilde* (revised edn., 1963). Subsequent references to Wilde's *Letters* are to this edition.

[2] Wilde, *Letters*, 490–1. This long letter was written in Reading Gaol in January–March 1897. An abridged version was published by Robert Ross in 1905 as *De Profundis*; the fullest version is that contained in *Letters*, 423–511.

in symbolic relations to the art and culture of my age', and in conversation with Gide he remarked that the great drama of his life
lay in his having put his talent into his works, and his genius into
his life.[3] For an author who returned as often as Wilde did to the
proposition that art transforms and is the superior of Nature, such
claims were more than boasting – they were an affirmation of
faith.

Oscar Wilde was born in Dublin on 16 October 1854, second
son of Sir William and Lady Wilde. The father was an eminent
surgeon, the mother a poetess and fervent Irish nationalist who
wrote as 'Speranza'. To medical distinction Sir William joined
notoriety as a philanderer.[4] Both parents were enthusiasts for the
study of Irish legend, folk-lore and history, an interest reflected in
the first two of the names given to their son, Oscar Fingal
O'Flahertie Wills Wilde. He was educated at Portora Royal
School and Trinity College, Dublin, where he became a protégé
of the classicist John Pentland Mahaffy. In 1875 he won a schol-
arship – a 'Classical Demyship' – to Magdalen College, Oxford,
where he subsequently took first-class honours in the final school
of *Literae Humaniores* (Greek and Roman literature, history and
philosophy). He picked up a reputation for wit, charm and conversational prowess. Most important, he came under the influence of two eminent writers on art and its relation to life, John
Ruskin and Walter Pater. Ruskin, the most distinguished contemporary art critic, championed the moral and social dimensions
of art, and its ability to influence men's lives for the better. Under
Ruskin's supervision, Wilde and a few other undergraduates had
begun the construction of a road near Hinksey, as a practical
demonstration of the aesthetic dignity of labour and the work-
manlike qualities essential to the labours of the artist. From Pater,
Wilde learned a conflicting interpretation of art as a means to the
cultivation of the individual, an idea which received its most
notorious statement in the 'Conclusion' to Pater's book, *The
Renaissance*. There the completely developed sensibility is
claimed as the expression of a full existence: 'To burn always
with this hard, gem-like flame, to maintain this ecstasy, is success
in life'.[5] These two theories of the relation between art and life
were to dominate Wilde's writing. The arguments of the painter
James McNeill Whistler against conservative critics' insistence on

---

[3] Wilde, *Letters*, 466; Gide, 'In Memoriam', ed. cit., 34.

[4] On Sir William and Lady Wilde, see Terence de Vere White, *Parents of Oscar
Wilde* (1967).

[5] Walter Pater, *The Renaissance* (1873; Library edn., 1910), 236. This 'Conclusion'
was omitted in the second edition (1877) and restored, in a modified form, in the
third edition (1888).

moral significance and pictorial verisimilitude in art also influenced Wilde deeply.[6] The close of his Oxford career was marked by two triumphs – his first-class degree and the Newdigate prize for his poem *Ravenna* – and two failures. Wilde was not given the Chancellor's English Essay Prize for his essay 'The Rise of Historical Criticism' and he was not offered a fellowship at Magdalen.

Moving to London, Wilde set about making himself a name in the capital's fashionable artistic and literary worlds. He had enough poems to make a collected volume, published at his own expense in 1881, and he was seen at the right parties, first nights and private views. Occasionally he wore the velvet coat and knee-breeches, soft-collared shirt and cravat, that became fixed in the popular imagination as 'aesthetic' dress (and which derived from a fancy-dress ball he had attended when an undergraduate). In December 1881 he embarked on a lecture-tour of the United States organized by the impresario Richard D'Oyly Carte. This was a shrewd back-up to the tour of Gilbert and Sullivan's comic opera *Patience*, but it was also a simple exploitation of the American appetite for being lectured to. Although *Patience*, which satirized the Aesthetic Movement, featured rival poets dressed in a costume closely resembling that adopted by Wilde, the lecturer was taken seriously as a prophet of the 'new renaissance' of art. In his lectures he insisted on comparing the new preoccupation with life-styles with the aspirations of the Italian Renaissance and the Romantic Movement – this was 'a sort of new birth of the spirit of man', like the earlier rebirth 'in its desire for a more gracious and comely way of life, its passion for physical beauty, its exclusive attention to form, its seeking for new subjects for poetry, new forms of art, new intellectual and imaginative enjoyment ...'[7] The blend of aesthetic theory and enthusiasm for reform of design and colouring in dress and decorative art was derived from a variety of sources, not all successfully synthesized. In addition to Ruskin, Pater and Whistler, Wilde had absorbed the ideas of William Morris and the architect E. W. Godwin. The lectures were exercises in *haute vulgarisation* and not all the sources were acknowledged. Japanese and other oriental art, eighteenth-century furniture, distempered walls in pastel colours, stylized floral motifs – all had made their appearance in English art before Wilde became their advocate. But the influence of his popu-

---

[6] Whistler later quarrelled with Wilde, accusing him of plagiarism. Some of their exchanges appeared in Whistler's *The Gentle Art of Making Enemies* (1890) and in *Wilde vs. Whistler* (1906).

[7] Wilde, 'The English Renaissance of Art', in Robert Ross's edition of his *Essays and Lectures* (1909), 111f. The text was edited by Ross from four drafts of a lecture given in New York on 9 January 1882.

larizing talents was, for all that, considerable. 'In fact,' wrote Max Beerbohm in 1895, looking back on 1880 as though it were a remote historical period, 'Beauty had existed long before 1880. It was Mr Oscar Wilde who managed her *début*.'[8]

As well as establishing him as a popular oracle on matters of art and taste Wilde's lecture-tour made him a great deal of badly-needed money – he had no prospect of inheriting a family fortune, and would have to make his own way. On his return the velvet suits were discarded, and his hair, worn long and flowing in his 'Aesthetic' period, was cut short in a style resembling the young Nero. The figure described by Gide was beginning to emerge. After a holiday in Paris, Wilde moved into rooms at 9 Charles Street, Grosvenor Square. He returned briefly to New York for the first performance of his melodrama *Vera; or, the Nihilists* and then pre-pared for an autumn lecture-tour of the United Kingdom. On 26 November he became engaged to Constance Lloyd, and they mar-ried on 29 May 1884. In January 1885 they moved into a house designed by Godwin at 16 Tite Street, Chelsea. Two sons, Cyril and Vyvyan, were born in 1885 and 1886 respectively. In the early years of his marriage Wilde was working hard as a journalist. He con-tributed reviews to magazines (including the *Pall Mall Gazette* and the *Dramatic Review*) and for a while even undertook the editor-ship of one, *Woman's World*, which he hoped to turn into 'the rec-ognized organ through which women of culture and position will express their views, and to which they will contribute'.[9] By and by Constance came into a small inheritance, but money was never plentiful. The life of a professional journalist was laborious and demanded a high degree of craftsmanship, but it offered a training from which Wilde, like Shaw, Wells, and many others, profited immensely. Wilde became a fastidious and tireless reviser of his own work, and his reviews show him as an acute critic of others.

In 1891 four of Wilde's books appeared, all consisting of earlier work, some of it in a revised form: *Intentions*, a collection of criti-cal essays; *Lord Arthur Savile's Crime and Other Stories*; *The Picture of Dorian Gray*, considerably altered from the version pub-lished in *Lippincott's Monthly Magazine* in 1890; and a collection of children's stories, *A House of Pomegranates*. In the same year a verse tragedy written in 1882, *The Duchess of Padua*, was pro-duced in New York by Lawrence Barrett under the title *Guido Ferranti*. Like *Vera* it was poorly received, but Wilde was already turning away from the pseudo-Elizabethan dramatic form that had preoccupied so many nineteenth-century poets and contemplating a newer, more commercially acceptable mode. In the summer of 1891

---

[8] Max Beerbohm, *Works* (1922), 39.

[9] Wilde, *Letters*, 202 (to Mrs Alfred Hunt, August, 1887).

he began work on the first of a series of successful plays for the fashionable theatres of the West End: *Lady Windermere's Fan* (St James's, 20 February 1892), *A Woman of No Importance* (Haymarket, 19 April 1893), *An Ideal Husband* (Haymarket, 3 January 1895) and *The Importance of Being Earnest* (St James's, 14 February 1895). The refusal of a performance licence to the exotic biblical tragedy *Salomé* (in 1892) proved merely a temporary setback: acclaim as a dramatic author confirmed Wilde's career in what seemed an irresistible upward curve.

The summer of 1891 was also remarkable for the beginning of an association that was to be the direct cause of Wilde's downfall: the poet Lionel Johnson introduced him to 'Bosie', Lord Alfred Douglas, the third son of the Marquess of Queensberry. Wilde appears to have been already a practising homosexual, and his marriage was under some strain. The affair with Douglas estranged him further from Constance, and the drain it caused on Wilde's nervous and financial resources was formidable. Douglas was happy to let Wilde spend money on him after his father stopped his allowance; more seriously, he made ceaseless demands on the time set aside for writing. In *De Profundis* Wilde described his attempts to finish *An Ideal Husband* in an apartment in St James's Place:

> I arrived ... every morning at 11.30, in order to have the opportunity of thinking and writing without the interruptions inseparable from my own household, quiet and peaceful as that household was. But the attempt was vain. At twelve o'clock you drove up, and stayed smoking cigarettes and chattering till 1.30, when I had to take you out to luncheon at the Café Royal or the Berkeley. Luncheon with its liqueurs lasted usually till 3.30. For an hour you retired to White's [Club]. At tea-time you appeared again, and stayed until it was time to dress for dinner. You dined with me either at the Savoy or at Tite Street. We did not separate as a rule till after midnight, as supper at Willis's had to wind up the entrancing day.[10]

This was in 1893. A year later Wilde was working on what was to prove his last play, *The Importance of Being Earnest*, the first draft of which had been composed during a family holiday (largely Douglas-free) at Worthing. In October Constance had returned to London with the children. Wilde and Douglas stayed together in Brighton, first at the Metropole Hotel, and then in private lodgings. Douglas developed influenza and Wilde nursed him through it. He in turn suffered an attack of the virus, and Douglas (by Wilde's account) more or less neglected him. The result was what seemed

[10] Wilde, *Letters*, 426.

like an irrevocable quarrel, with Douglas living at Wilde's expense in a hotel but hardly bothering to visit him. In hindsight Wilde claimed that this cruelty afforded him a moment of clear understanding:

> Is it necessary for me to state that I saw clearly that it would be a dishonour to myself to continue even an acquaintance with such a one as you had showed yourself to be? That I recognized that ultimate moment had come, and recognized it as being really a great relief? And that I knew that for the future my Art and Life would be freer and better and more beautiful in every possible way? Ill as I was, I felt at ease.[11]

But reconciliation followed.

On 3 January 1895 *An Ideal Husband* was given its first performance. Meanwhile George Alexander, actor-manager of the St James's Theatre, had turned down *The Importance of Being Earnest*. It found a taker in Charles Wyndham, who intended to bring it out at the Criterion. Then Alexander found himself at a loss for a play to replace Henry James's *Guy Domville*, which had failed spectacularly. Wyndham agreed to release *The Importance of Being Earnest* on the condition that he had the option on Wilde's next play, and it was put into rehearsal at the St James's. At first Wilde attended rehearsals, but his continual interruptions made Alexander suggest that he might leave the manager and his company to their own resources. He agreed with good grace and left with Douglas for a holiday in Algeria. There they encountered André Gide, who was told by Wilde that he had a premonition of some disaster awaiting him on his return.[12] Although his artistic reputation was beyond question, and he was shortly to have two plays running simultaneously in the West End, Wilde was already worried by the activities of Douglas's father. Queensberry was a violent, irrational man, who hated his son's lover and who was capable of hurting both parties. Bosie insisted on flaunting his relationship with Wilde to annoy his father and he was reckless of the effect of this public display of unconventional behaviour. Homosexuality was no less a fact of life in 1895 than it is now; moreover, the artistic and theatrical world accommodated it better than society at large. It had a flourishing and varied subculture and a number of sophisticated apologists. The double life that it entailed was by no means a simple matter of

---

[11] Wilde, *Letters*, 438.

[12] 'I am not claiming that Wilde clearly saw prison rising up before him; but I do assert that the dramatic turn which surprised and astounded London, abruptly turning Wilde from accuser to accused, did not, strictly speaking, cause him any surprises' (Gide, 'In Memoriam', ed. cit., 34).

deceit and guilt for Wilde: it suited the cultivation of moral independence and detachment from society that he considered essential to art. None the less, if his affair with Douglas should ever come to be more public, and if the law were to be invoked, Wilde would be ruined. There had been scandals and trials involving homosexuals of the upper classes, which had to a degree closed their ranks to protect their own. But Wilde had made powerful enemies in a country whose leaders, institutions and press seemed devoted to Philistinism and where art itself was always suspect as constituting a threat to the moral fibre of the nation. *Dorian Gray* in particular had aroused violent mistrust, especially in its original form, and a satirical novel by Robert Hichens, *The Green Carnation* (1894), had hinted at a homosexual relationship between two characters obviously based on Wilde and Douglas. Queensberry had made his feelings about his son's private life well known in Clubland. On the first night of *The Importance of Being Earnest*, which opened on 14 February 1895, he tried to cause a disturbance at the theatre, but was thwarted by the management. The play was a great success – according to one of the actors, 'The audience rose in their seats and cheered and cheered again'.[13] As it settled down to what promised to be a long run, Wilde's career was at its height.

A fortnight later, on 28 February, Queensberry left a card at the Albemarle Club 'For Oscar Wilde posing as a somdomite' [*sic*]. The club porter put the card in an envelope, noting on the back the time and date, and Wilde was given it when he arrived at the club later that evening. The events that followed ruined him within a few months. Urged on by Douglas, but against the advice of most of his friends, Wilde sued Queensberry for criminal libel. The case went against Wilde, who found himself answering charges under the 1885 Criminal Law Amendment Act, which made both private and public homosexual relations between men illegal. Significantly, the accusations against him did not include his affair with Douglas: he was alleged to have committed acts of gross indecency on a number of occasions and to have conspired to procure the committing of such acts. The men involved were 'renters', young, lower-class, male prostitutes, and there was a strong sense in the proceedings that Wilde was being tried for betraying his class's social as well as sexual ethics. Much was made of the alleged immorality of his works, especially *Dorian Gray*. The jury at what was effectively the second trial of Wilde (after the hearings in his charge against Queensberry) failed to agree, and a retrial was ordered. Finally, on 25 May 1895, Wilde was convicted and sentenced to two years' imprisonment with hard labour. In the autumn he was declared

---

[13] Allen Aynesworth, quoted by Hesketh Pearson, *The Life of Oscar Wilde* (1946), 257.

bankrupt and all his effects were auctioned, including drafts and manuscripts of published and unpublished works. On 19 May 1897 he was released and took up residence in France. During his imprisonment he had composed a long, bitter letter to Douglas, later published under the title *De Profundis*. Shortly after his release he completed a narrative poem, *The Ballad of Reading Gaol*. These and a few letters to the press on prison reform apart, Wilde published nothing new after his imprisonment. He did manage to arrange for the publication of *The Importance of Being Earnest* and *An Ideal Husband* in 1899. Projects for further plays came to nothing. The affair with Douglas was taken up again and continued sporadically. They led a nomadic life on the Continent, Wilde often chronically in debt despite the good offices of his friends. His allowance from Constance was withdrawn when he resumed living with Bosie. His plays were not yet being revived in England, and what little royalties his published works brought in went to creditors.

Wilde died on 30 November 1900 in Paris, from cerebral meningitis which set in after an operation on his ear. The day before he had been received into the Roman Catholic Church. He was buried at Bagneux, but in 1909 his remains were moved to the Père Lachaise cemetery, where they now rest under a monument by Jacob Epstein.

R.J.

The Play

Lady Windermere's Fan was first staged by George Alexander at the St James's Theatre on 20 February 1892. The play became an immediate success and that success became material for anecdotes about its author, who had been living in the public eye, a prototype of a modern media personality, for over a decade. Press reports of the first night described how, after the applause had died down, the audience called for the author. According to the *Sunday Times* Wilde appeared on stage nonchalantly smoking and told the audience 'I think that you have enjoyed the performance as much as I have, and I am pleased to believe that you like the piece almost as much as I do myself.'[14] The anecdote illustrates both the reputation for boldness and insouciant wit which Wilde enjoyed in the early 1890s, and the sense of occasion for which first nights at the St James's were celebrated. The theatre was then beginning to acquire its reputation for a reportoire that reflected and endorsed the *mores*

[14] *Sunday Times*, 21 February 1892, 5.

and tastes of its audience, predominantly those of the upper-middle classes residing in or near St James's, Mayfair and Belgravia which the manager of the St James's Theatre, George Alexander, wished to attract.[15] The play ran for 156 performances. It was then taken on a short provincial tour and returned to London to run until early December 1892. *Lady Windermere's Fan* made Wilde a small fortune. For example, the St James's account sheets show that in the week ending 11 March 1892, the play's total gross was £646 2s. 6d. Wilde's royalty was 5% on the first £600 and 7.5% thereafter; for that week he received in total £43 15s. 1d. for 6 performances. Later weeks tell a similar story. The figures for the week ending 25 March 1892 reveal that the play grossed £663 18s. 6d., and that Wilde earned £46 12s. 5d.; by July he was still earning almost £50 a week in royalties. These were large sums for a writer who only a few years earlier had earned a living by reviewing for one or two pounds an article.[16]

Critics were less certain than the first-night audience in their reception of the play. Most acknowledged the brilliance of Wilde's dialogue as the play's most distinctive and admirable feature; some dwelt on its structural similarities to recent French and British drama. The most hostile review, that by the arch-conservative Clement Scott in the *Illustrated London News* (27 February 1892), criticized the play on the grounds that it did not depict London Society as accurately as other recent pieces of Society Drama. Scott's observation goes to the heart of the play. The term 'Society' appears on several occasions in the play and is central to it. Today critics would interpret Scott's reading as a sociological one, although how they understand and value Wilde's representation of his society is very different. More precisely, the alleged 'misrepresentation' which Scott dwelt upon is translated by modern critical analysis into a discussion of the operation of power in late nineteenth-century British society.

In fact for the first seventy years of the twentieth century, it was more usual for critics to discuss the play's moral issues in isolation from its social reference; so *Lady Windermere's Fan* was affiliated to a tradition of drama which dealt with what were supposed to be universal moral concerns. Moreover within that tradition it was

---

[15] There is, however, quite a lot of evidence that some members of the London working classes did attend West-End entertainments. See Joseph W. Donohue, Jr., 'Recent Studies of Oscar Wilde', *Nineteenth Century Theatre*, 16, 2 (1988), 123–36.

[16] In pre-decimal coinage, one shilling (1s.) was 5 new pence; 2.4 old pennies (2.4d.) were equivalent to one new penny. To give a context to Wilde's earnings from the play: £80 per year would have represented a good working-class wage; the lowest middle class salary (for, say, a clerk) was between £75 and a £120 per year.

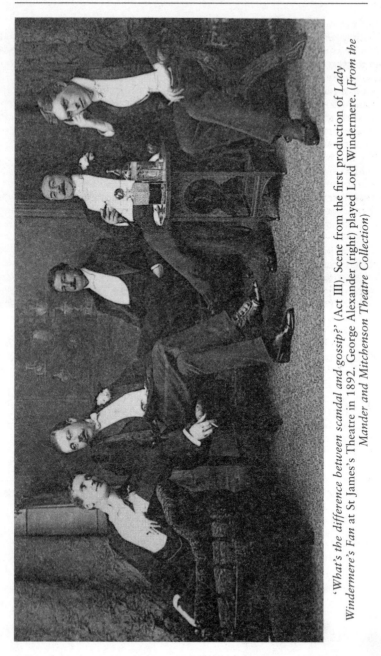

'What's the difference between scandal and gossip?' (Act III). Scene from the first production of *Lady Windermere's Fan* at St James's Theatre in 1892. George Alexander (right) played Lord Windermere. (*From the Mander and Mitchenson Theatre Collection*)

held to be a minor play because the moral issue which it did discuss
– that of sexual equality – had by 1892 become something of a
cliché of Victorian melodrama. It is worth remembering that the
main interest of feminists in the 1890s had moved from the domestic to the more overtly public and political: the right to vote, to
employment, to education. By contrast the conflict between an obligation to self and an obligation to family, or between duty and
desire, which forms the moral centre of *Lady Windermere's Fan*,
had been the concern of an earlier generation of women writers,
and can be found in any number of mid-Victorian novels, plays and
poetry. More recent revaluations of *Lady Windermere's Fan*, based
on a renewed sociological understanding of its reference, emphasize
the ironic distance between the morality of the play as whole (and
therefore that of its author), and the specific moral decisions made
by the characters. The blurred morality which early critics (such as
Scott) had seen as a weakness becomes a strength if Wilde is understood to be contesting the conventions which he is using, particularly the moral essentialism on which Victorian melodrama
invariably relies.

This view of Wilde as a dramatist who wished to subvert the rep-
resentational functions or qualities of late nineteenth-century
Society Drama requires an understanding of the complex social and
artistic milieux in which his plays were first performed. That understanding can usefully begin with the meanings of the term which
Scott uses – 'Society': more exactly, what Society is in the play, and
what it is in relation to the individuals who first saw the play – the
dazzled first-night audience at the St James's for whom Wilde had
written it. The phrase 'London Society', and its more emphatic
forms 'Good Society' or 'Best Society', were understood by the late
nineteenth century as simply an élite of the most distinguished figures of the nation – distinguished, that is, by political, social and
cultural fame, but first and foremost by birth. The justification for
the existence of such an élite was rarely, if ever, questioned by its
members. Wilde knew this well, and in his next play, *A Woman of
No Importance*, he has Lord Illingworth emphatically tell the young
Gerald Arbuthnot:

> To be in it is merely a bore. But to be out of it simply a tragedy.
> Society is a necessary thing. No man has any real success in this
> world unless he has got women to back him, and women rule
> society.[17]

Or as Lady Bracknell tells Algernon in *The Importance of Being
Earnest*:

---

[17] *A Woman of No Importance*, III, 78–81 (CW, 460).

Never speak disrespectfully of Society, Algernon. Only people who can't get into it do that.[18]

A modern sociologist would understand the term 'Society' as referring to a status or interest group regulated by an elaborately coded system of relationships, the main function of which was to provide solidarity and cohesion, as well as to assign position and rank to its members. It was, like all other status groups (as Lord Illingworth in Wilde's play amply knows) almost obsessively concerned with access to or exclusion from its ranks. Indeed, social ostracism, including the ostracism of Mrs Erlynne from London Society in *Lady Windermere's Fan*, was a common theme in nineteenth-century literature and drama. During the course of the nineteenth century, Society developed an elaborate series of social occasions, the informally but rigorously policed and exclusive London Season to which Dumby and the Duchess of Berwick refer in Act II. The Season was a pattern of social events which included not only private entertainments (like Lady Windermere's ball) but public events like Ascot, Henley and the Private View of the Royal Academy. The central feature of Society, making the exclusiveness of its social events possible, was a tightly regulated code of behaviour which, as much as money or birth, was the defining attribute of Society's members, for it identified them publicly as *ladies* and *gentlemen*. To deviate from these conventions (as Wilde's heroines do – Mrs Erlynne in *Lady Windermere's Fan*, and Mrs Arbuthnot in *A Woman of No Importance*), was to relinquish that title and the distinction it bestowed and to place oneself outside Society.

The rigid codification of what constituted acceptable behaviour regulated both domestic and social life; as a consequence it produced an intense feeling of community. And so a striking feature of Society Drama is the theme of the social acceptability or otherwise of those characters who do not conform to Society's *mores*. The minute regulation of domestic life in the last half of the nineteenth century was publicly advertised as etiquette, the rules of which constituted an elaborate ceremonial governing all social occasions, public and private. Etiquette, because it controlled domestic and social life rather than commercial or public life, was formalized by women: responsibility for its observation or its policing became peculiarly their province. As its rules were internalized, so they became legitimated as 'natural'. Two claims were made for etiquette as a code of practice: that it could be justified by commonsense, and that it was fundamentally 'natural' courtesy, refined by tradition. Nineteenth-century publishers produced a veritable library of books describing what counted as acceptable behaviour

[18] *The Importance of Being Earnest*, III, 188–9 (CW, 374).

for the aspiring entrant to the world of London Society. One such popular work claimed that:

> Our present code of etiquette is constructed upon the refinement, polish, and culture of years, of centuries. Wealth and luxury, and contact with all that is beautiful in art and nature, have in all ages exercised a powerful influence on the manners of men ... The word etiquette ... must be viewed in a double light, and be taken from a moral point as well as from a conventional one. A kindly nature, and an unselfish spirit are never wanting in true politeness, but the conventionalities of society give the finish and completeness to the whole.[19]

The assertion that there is no real disjunction between morals and manners, between what London's élite did and what it said it did, is one of Wilde's principal themes in *Lady Windermere's Fan*. At the play's centre is an exploration of the possible anatagonism between what was claimed for etiquette as the ethical and social code of London Society and what observing it could actually entail. It is precisely here that the ironic distance between the morality of the play as whole and the specific moral decisions of individual characters, which I mentioned earlier, becomes clear. This ironic distance is taken as evidence by some critics that Wilde saw the behaviour of London's élite as a matter of power, and therefore of politics, rather than of morality.

In order to understand these observations more fully, we need to return to the role which Victorian theatre played within its culture. One of its most striking features was its faithful reflection and endorsement of social class. Issues of class affected every aspect of theatrical production – the building and furnishing of theatres, audience composition, censorship regulations, box-office receipts, reviews and even the content of particular plays. This was particularly true of middle-class influence, because it was largely middle-class patronage which financed the growth of the West-End theatre for which Wilde wrote in the last quarter of the nineteenth century (a middle-class which was then a much smaller proportion of the population than it is today). Theatre building had been funded by the increased disposable income of the middle-classes, and the luxury and taste which characterized the newly refurbished West-End theatres were specifically directed at a middle class clientèle Indeed, Victorian West-End theatre can usefully be thought of as forming part of a larger social round. The theatre offered London Society a largely favourable reflection of itself and of its values; and Society responded by incorporating this theatrical experience into

---

[19] *Manners and Rules*, p. 3.

its own norms of behaviour – so much so that 'going to the theatre' became by the last quarter of the century an important social event, one in which the audience, as much as the actors, were on display.

An important consequence was the way in which the values of London Society informed the representation of moral and social issues on the commercial stage. In general terms, moral debates in Society Drama were limited: rather than question the relative merits of one or more courses of action, they restricted themselves to debating how the *given* morals of a particular class are to be enforced. So for the majority of dramatists, and particularly for writers such as Henry Arthur Jones and Arthur Wing Pinero, the main concern was with the fair implementation of a morality: its existence as a guide to right conduct was never questioned. In this sense, Society Drama more often than not became one of the external confirmations of the social values that London Society had normalized. Society Drama used relatively few motifs and situations. The plays posed familiar moral problems, particularly problems of sexual morality, and resolved them in ways which confirmed the ethics of their audience. The plots of most plays are therefore easily summarized: they concern young men's responsibility for class and country; or the efforts of *parvenus* or *déclassés* to penetrate London Society by marriage; or the familiar figure of 'a woman with a past' – a woman (like Mrs Erlynne) whose former sexual conduct disqualifies her from polite society and whose guilty secrets are inevitably revealed during the course of the play. Many of these staple elements find their way into *Lady Windermere's Fan*.

As I have suggested, one such staple is the relationship between marriage and class. The exclusiveness and rigidity of the English class system had been an important topic for fiction from the 1840s onwards. Some of the most familiar examples are Benjamin Disraeli's *Sybil* (1845), Elizabeth Gaskell's *Mary Barton* (1848), Charles Dickens's *Our Mutual Friend* (1864–5), George Eliot's *Middlemarch* (1871–2), and Thomas Hardy's *Tess of the D'Urbervilles* (1891). Largely because of the different nature of its audiences, the theatre discussed these themes less thoroughly and turned to them only in the final decades of the century. Society Drama was not concerned with relationships between classes but, as I have noted, with situations and dilemmas within one class. In particular, it was concerned with that familiar solvent of class differences in Victorian fiction, marriage. As Mrs Erlynne in *Lady Windermere's Fan* knows, the social institution of marriage was one of the most effective ways of moving across social and class barriers and of gaining (in her case of regaining) access to London Society. The consequences of wise and unwise marriages are a constant theme in Society Drama, and the way in which Society policed itself is a recurrent motif. By the 1890s a number of playwrights were attempting to present the subject of sexual equality in a more open, modern way. Class and marriage formed the subject of Arthur Wing Pinero's highly successful *The Second Mrs Tanqueray*, which George Alexander staged at the St James's in 1893 shortly after *Lady Windermere's Fan* had been taken off. More specifically, there was a group of plays which raised the issue of Society's unequal treatment of men and women, and some reviewers saw Wilde's play belonging to this group. The theme of equality was rehearsed in Henry Arthur Jones's *The Case of Rebellious Susan* (Criterion, 1894) and *Mrs Dane's Defence* (Wyndham's, 1900), as well as in Pinero's *The Notorious Mrs Ebbsmith* (Garrick, 1895). Jones's characters reiterate the familiar Victorian conviction that sexual inequality was somehow 'natural': as here in *Rebellious Susan*:

ELAINE SHRIMPTON
Do you deny that Woman has been most shamefully treated by Man?
SIR RICHARD KATO
It isn't Man that's ungallant to Woman. It's Nature that is so ungallant and so unkind to your sex.
ELAINE SHRIMPTON
We will correct Nature.
SIR RICHARD KATO
By changing your sex? What is it that you ladies want? You are evidently dissatisfied with being women. You cannot wish to be anything so brutal and disgusting as a man. And unfortunately there is no neuter sex in the human species.[20]

or here, in *Mrs Dane's Defence*:

SIR DANIEL CARTERET
A man demands the treasure of a woman's purest love. It's what he buys and pays for with the strength of his arm and the sweat of his brow. It's the condition on which he makes her his wife and fights the world for her and his children. It's his fiercest instinct, and he does well to guard it; for it's the very mainspring of a nation's health and soundness.[21]

This idea of the 'naturalness' of a specific sexual ethic is a question which Wilde raises in *Lady Windermere's Fan*. In fact his interest in the topic of sexual equality pre-dates the play. In May 1889 in the periodical *Woman's World* (which he then edited) he reviewed a book entitled *Darwinism and Politics* (1889) by David Ritchie; he agreed with Ritchie that different sexual ethics could not be justified

---

[20] Henry Arthur Jones, *The Case of Rebellious Susan* (1899), 100.
[21] Henry Arthur Jones, *Mrs Dane's Defence* (1905), 109.

by an appeal to the biological differences between men and women. Wilde argued that 'the cultivation of separate sorts of virtues and separate ideals of duty in men and women has led to the whole social fabric being weaker and unhealthier than it need be.'[22] While such views appear liberal enough, we should be careful not to make Wilde too much of a champion of women's rights. He was more than happy, should the occasion demand, to allow characters to mock feminist opinions, and it is noticeable that in *Lady Windermere's Fan* the character who most forcefully advocates equality is Lord Darlington, the dandy/seducer. Indeed Wilde's plays in general are much more conservative than his critical writing; *An Ideal Husband*, for example, enjoins very separate roles for men and women. This apparent discrepancy might not be simply a matter of 'bad faith' on Wilde's part. It might rather be a consequence of the constraints which governed dramatic authorship as opposed to the relative freedom of journalism.

Closely related to – indeed forming part of – this topic of sexual equality was that of adultery and the breakdown of marriage. Once again the theme was a stock element of Society Drama, although it was unusual for the subject to be so central to a play as it is to *Lady Windermere's Fan*. Adultery and divorce were extremely topical issues: they were at the centre of a wide debate about marriage and marriage legislation at the beginning of the 1890s. We ought to remind ourselves of the fact that despite a number of reforms, the laws governing marriage in the late nineteenth century continued to discriminate against the interests of women. Legislation, such as the Married Woman's Property Acts, which entitled married women to become legal agents controlling money and possessing property, had only gradually been put in place over a number of years. Similarly, nineteenth-century legislation on divorce (which had created civil divorce for the first time in English history in 1857) was so one-sided that most women were still effectively trapped inside marriage. Particular cases (such as the Mackenzie Divorce Case, begun in 1891) began to interpret more liberally what constituted cruelty by a husband and therefore what was legally justifiable desertion by the wife. That said, however, the standard by which the marital conduct of men and women was judged was still highly unequal: Lady Windermere's desertion of her husband, child and home would still have been considered far more damaging than her husband's supposed philandering. Exactly the same double standard is the subject of much late nineteenth-century fiction. Hardy's *Tess* is 'punished' for a premarital sexual relationship in a way that no male character is: sexual knowledge and experience for men and women were still valued very differently. In Act III Lord

[22] Oscar Wilde, *Reviews*, 488.

Windermere's friends joke about the attractions of a woman with a past – that is, a sexually experienced woman; but for Lady Windermere such conduct (particularly if she were to be to be discovered in a man's rooms) would be catastrophic.

In early drafts of the play the opening act quite clearly sets out to renegotiate what the sexual 'purity' of Lady Windermere means; these drafts contrast her unyielding puritan morality with the flagrant immorality of the world in which she moves. Lord Windermere's relationship with Mrs Erlynne is revealed to be a straightforward attempt to protect his wife from potentially contagious contact with a sexually compromised and blackmailing woman. (The offensiveness of a bad woman to the good was a familiar theme in Society Drama, and one example of it, Lady Windermere's resolute desire that Mrs Erlynne should not be invited to her ball, is retained in the performed and published versions of the play). This conventionalized opening, where good and bad are set in a simple and stark opposition, contrasts strikingly with Wilde's early ideas about the play's ending, where the 'purity' of Lady Windermere is eventually shown to be a lie that can only be maintained publicly by deceit. Mrs Erlynne, disgraced and excluded as she is, now becomes a scapegoat, and her reputation is 'sacrificed' to save Lady Windermere's honour. In any meaningful sense, she, the stereotypical villainess, is ultimately judged to be as good as the nominally 'pure' Lady Windermere. In this way, the play's early working title, 'A Good Woman', exemplifies its initial theme, for in its early form the play sets out a conflict in which we learn that the conventionalized categories of good and bad (with respect to sexual ethics) cannot be defined with any certainty. As such, the themes of these early drafts of the play can be seen to form part of a pattern familiar from Wilde's early criticism, particularly the essays in *Intentions* (1891), where he attempts to redefine accepted values and ethics.

This line of argument would suggest that in the play's first drafts there is a strong implication that London Society's code of sexual ethics was founded on hypocrisy, as well as an implication that 'purity' is itself only a form of self-deceit, albeit a socially sanctioned one. Such an interpretation has the further advantage of fitting pleasingly with what we know about Wilde's own double life at this time. In 1892 Wilde gave the appearance of being a happily married Victorian father; in reality he was leading a homosexual double life – in his own phrase, 'feasting with panthers'. In the first drafts of the play, Mrs Erlynne ruthlessly exploits these double standards of morality in order to re-enter London Society. The play's opening suggests that her attempt to blackmail Lord Windermere is only possible given a corrupt and hypocritical society, one for which respectability – which in the play's (and Society's) terms means good parentage – must be preserved at all costs. In other words, Mrs Erlynne's motives might be corrupt, but the corruption of London Society is deeper. It is tempting to argue, then, that the play as Wilde initially conceived it was radical for the London stage of the early 1890s.

By the time the Licensing Copy was submitted to the Lord Chamberlain's Office, however, Wilde had made a number of significant alterations to these early drafts. Mrs Erlynne became a character much less single-mindedly concerned with money and position, to the extent that the sacrifice of her social ambitions for the sake of her daughter becomes more plausible. Further changes, which have serious implications for how we understand Mrs Erlynne's character, were made after the first performance. In the earliest drafts, the real identity of Mrs Erlynne is not revealed until the play's final scenes. At some early point in the play's genesis Wilde's manager, George Alexander, concluded that there was dramatic advantage to be gained from disclosing to the audience in either Act I or Act II that Mrs Erlynne and Lady Windermere are related, mother and daughter. Alexander's biographer, the playwright A. E. W. Mason, maintains that Wilde was initially unhappy to make the change and quotes a letter from Alexander to Wilde where he emphasizes the benefits which would follow from the change:

> I am perfectly certain, too, that for the good of the play the audience should know very early in the second act, or at any rate at the end of it, that Mrs Erlynne is the mother – this too I have impressed upon you over and over again, but you have refused even to discuss it. The interest would be increased by this knowledge and Mrs Erlynne and Lord Windermere would not be in a false position.[23]

The tone of the letter ('this too I have impressed upon you over and over again') implies disagreements between manager and author, and these were to resurface when Alexander staged Wilde's last play, *The Importance of Being Earnest*. However, it is clear that on both occasions Alexander's instinct for better theatrical practice prevailed; the end of the second act of *Lady Windermere's Fan* was indeed changed, but not until after the first night. It seems that it was not until a public performance of the play that Wilde conceded the rightness of Alexander's judgement. In fact Wilde subsequently wrote to the *St James's Gazette* denying that the change had been made because of adverse critical comment about the play's structure:

> I am bound to state that all my friends, without exception, were of opinion that the psychological interest of the second act would be

---

[23] A. E. W. Mason, *Sir George Alexander and the St James's Theatre* (1935), 37–8.

greatly increased by the disclosure of the actual relationship existing between Lady Windermere and Mrs Erlynne – an opinion, I may add, that had been held strongly and urged by Mr Alexander.[24]

Moreover, Wilde kept Alexander's suggested revision of the revelation of Mrs Erlynne's identity when he came to put together the first book edition of the play. (Similarly he kept Alexander's changes when he prepared the book version of *The Importance of Being Earnest* in 1899.)

Once Mrs Erlynne has been revealed to the audience as Lady Windermere's mother, the dramatic impetus of the play changes, in the sense that the radical emphasis on hypocrisy in society which characterized the first two acts is replaced by the less challenging concentration on the tensions of a mother/daughter relationship. By explaining Mrs Erlynne's ambitions and motives in terms of maternal instinct, rather than in terms of a ruthless exploition of social hypocrisy, the play's original radicalism may seem to become muted. It is tempting, then, to argue from the evidence of the earliest drafts of the play, and up to its first performance, where Mrs Erlynne is more obviously a ruthless blackmailer, and where her identity as Lady Windermere's mother is withheld until the final act, that Wilde was intending to use his play to challenge contemporary views about equality, divorce and adultery. However, the history of the revisions to the play is more complex than this simple if appealing narrative, of a move from 'radicalism' to 'conservatism', would suggest.

It is true that in what appear to be the earliest drafts of the play information about Mrs Erlynne's identity is withheld until the last act. It is also true that the last drafts (and almost certainly the first-night prompt-copy) keep Mrs Erlynne's identity a secret until Act IV. However, there is a 'middle' group of drafts of the play which reveal it at the end of both Acts I and II. Clearly, then, differences of opinion about the revelation of Mrs Erlynne's identity had been going on for some time, and were not simply the result of any last minute change of mind.[25] Furthermore, the play's radicalism is not wholly compromised by this early revelation, and Wilde's claim that the change was made to enhance the piece's 'psychological

---

[24] *Letters*, 313. H. Montgomery Hyde suggests that the change was made after four or five performances (see H. Montgomery Hyde, *Oscar Wilde* (1976), 138). In his correspondence, Wilde seems to hint at a change after the first night, a detail since corroborated by Joel H. Kaplan. See Joel H. Kaplan, 'A Puppet's Power: George Alexander, Clement Scott, and the Replotting of *Lady Windermere's Fan*', *Theatre Notebook*, 46, 2 (1992), 59–73.

[25] The relationship between the drafts and the first edition is discussed more fully in 'The Play and its Drafts', below.

interest', rather than representing some form of political compromise, has considerable validity. Certainly the play's themes *are* changed by our knowledge of Mrs Erlynne's identity. After the disclosure of who she is, the 'point' of her protection of Lady Windermere in Act III is no longer to suggest that the same fundamental frailties exist in both 'good' and 'bad' women. Mrs Erlynne becomes much more than a fallen woman recognizing two basic social truths, that the *appearance* of morality and purity must be maintained at all costs, by deceit if necessary, and that deceit itself is justified by the hypocrisy of the society in which she lives. As Mrs Erlynne is revealed to be a mother, so the scene takes on a character much more usual in Victorian melodrama – that of a parent protecting a child. As a consequence, rather than evoke sympathy for the social outcast or the social victim (a theme common in Wilde's short fiction) the play becomes more guarded in its social criticism. The revised play, then, does set the selflessness of parental love against the selfish and destructive nature of sexual love. These too are familiar themes elsewhere in Wilde's work, and the change has the effect of making individual behaviour as much a moral as a social issue. However, the conviction that there is some essential relationship between deceit – acting a part – and the demands of public morality was *not* lost to the play. Rather it was displaced on to another group of characters, the play's dandies – principally Cecil Graham, Dumby and Lord Darlington. (In fact the development of Darlington's character through the remaining drafts, make him more complex than simple villain or dandy). Significantly the invention of Graham and Dumby, who take over the critical role of Darlington, seems to occur in those middle drafts – that is, at precisely the moment when Wilde first considered revealing Mrs Erlynne's real identity in Act II. In the other words, there is evidence that Wilde was fully in control of the play's themes, and was aware of the problems involved in trying to balance dramatic tension with a radical politics.

These three characters (Graham, Dumby and Darlington) belong to a much larger group central to Wilde's other work; they are seen most threateningly in Lord Henry Wotton in *The Picture of Dorian Gray* (1891) and most entertainingly in Algernon and Jack in *The Importance of Being Earnest* (performed 1895, published 1899). What is so significant about Lord Henry and his fictional relations is their freedom to flout social conventions. In the plays, however, this freedom is more limited: Wilde's dramatic dandies are free only to *talk about* breaking moral codes. The freedom which Lord Darlington or Lord Goring (in *An Ideal Husband*, performed 1895, published 1899) or Lord Illingworth (in *A Woman of No Importance*, performed 1893, published 1894) enjoy is that of verbal play. Verbally their freedom is absolute and is exercised through Wilde's own favourite conversational device, the paradox.

What characterizes the speech of the dandy is its insincerity and its contrivance; effect, rather than truth, is its intention. As such it confirms Wilde's own views about the laws of art. Through a series of highly contrived speeches, Darlington, and later Graham and Dumby, challenge the moral and social expectations of their audience, both on and off the stage. Their flippancies work by exposing the banality and moral complacency of Victorian drawing-room conversation. The consequences of this verbal iconoclasm, however, *are* restricted. Darlington can utter or hint at immoral sentiments; but he is forbidden to act immorally, for as soon as he actually breaks Society's moral code (in declaring his adulterous love for Lady Windermere), he abandons the pose of the dandy, and to all intents and purposes, ceases to have any significant critical function for the rest of the play. However, in Act III, as I have said, the dandy's role (and the social critique which it embodies) is passed to Cecil Graham and Dumby; their wit balances Darlington's reversion to a conventional melodramatic type, that of the disappointed lover.

Wilde's dandies ruthlessly exploit a feature of behaviour present to a lesser extent in all the other characters of the play – a willingness to lie. All social intercourse in *Lady Windermere's Fan* seems to work by the convention that an individual character modifies his or her speech in accordance with the expectations of his or her interlocutor. The Duchess of Berwick maintains that her nieces do not talk scandal, but merely 'remark' on what they see 'to everyone'. Lady Jedburgh's nephew, too, is destined for political success because he 'thinks like a Tory and talks like a Radical'. The smooth operation of London Society, with its series of regulated and accepted excuses, is seen to depend upon lies. So the Duchess of Berwick employs a variety of verbal masquerades to ensnare Hopper, with his newly-acquired colonial wealth, as a son-in-law. The Season, too, in Wilde's eyes, both requires and sanctions a variety of verbal deceptions for its success. The polite and successful social tattle at Lady Windermere's ball requires verbal inconsistencies (which in other situations become intended or unwitting lies):

DUMBY
> Good evening, Lady Stutfield. I suppose this will be the last ball of the season?

LADY STUTFIELD
> I suppose so, Mr Dumby. It's been a delightful season, hasn't it?

DUMBY
> Quite delightful. Good evening, Duchess. I suppose this will be the last ball of the season?

THE DUCHESS OF BERWICK
> I suppose so, Mr Dumby. It has been a very dull season, hasn't it?

DUMBY
> Dreadfully dull! Dreadfully dull!

MRS COWPER-COWPER

Good evening, Mr Dumby. I suppose this will be the last ball of the season?

DUMBY

Oh, I think not. There'll probably be two more.[26]

Indeed, there are only two characters in the play who make consistent attempts at truthfulness: Lady Windermere, who is finally reduced to a form of lying – withholding from Lord Windermere the truth about her presence in Lord Darlington's rooms; and Lord Augustus, who in his attempts to express what he feels is often reduced to mere inarticulacy. The implication of Wilde's emphasis on this particular aspect of London Society is that his dandies not only exploit, but perfect, a feature of social life already present in their world. Wilde's dandies act a role constantly and their performances are consequently more successful than those of their peers. In fact Wilde was only taking to extremes an accepted feature of etiquette. When contemporary manuals of conversation discussed the relationship between truthfulness and successful social intercourse, they were usually ambivalent. In this respect unusually frank advice was offered by J. P. Mahaffy in his *The Principles of the Art of Conversation* (1887) – a work all the more interesting because Mahaffy was Wilde's old tutor at Trinity College, Dublin. Ideally, Mahaffy maintained, conversation should combine entertainment, moral edification and truthfulness: 'the most solid and lasting recreation [and] the most excellent refreshment of the soul'.[27] In practice, he observed, there would invariably be a tension between truthfulness and social entertainment. In such cases, he advised, the most accomplished conversationalist should aim at entertaining his audience. So Mahaffy's manual at times endorses some of the observations and precepts of Lord Darlington and Cecil Graham:

But on the other hand, there is such a thing in society ... as being over-scrupulous in truthfulness. Even a consummate liar, though generally vulgar, and therefore offensive, is a better ingredient in company than the scrupulously truthful man, who weighs every statement, questions every fact, and corrects every inaccuracy. I have heard a witty talker pronounce it the golden rule of conversation *to know nothing accurately*.[28]

---

[26] See II, 14–25.

[27] J. P. Mahaffy, *The Principles of the Art of Conversation* (1887), 158–9.

[28] ibid., 78. The importance of effect rather than accuracy is a sentiment often expressed in Wilde's plays.

Yolanda Vasquez as Lady Windermere and Giles Havergal as Lord Windermere in Philip Prowse's 1988 production at the Glasgow Citizens Theatre. Photograph by John Vere Brown.

As a consequence Mahaffy – like Graham, Dumby and the Duchess of Berwick's nieces – realized the social attractions of gossip and the inevitability of scandal, which 'is deeply interesting to almost everybody, and though by no means improving is always entertaining'.[29] Wilde's dandies have, in a sense, assimilated advice like that offered by Mahaffy, for with them conversation has become an art; consequently the form and the effect of an utterance are its most important aspects. But in so doing, they merely reduce to absurdity a principle which Wilde saw as central to the operation of London Society – the socially effective, and so socially acceptable, lie. As Mrs Erlynne ruthlessly exploits the essential deceitfulness of Society's sexual ethics, so Wilde's dandies absurdly exploit the paradoxes of Society's social ethics. The play itself finally endorses some kinds of concealment not only as considerate and unselfish but also as necessary.

Finally, of course, all these potential contradictions in Society's values are reconciled by the play's happy ending. It is, however, a very partial justice which prevails in the last scene. Lady Windermere's honour is preserved, while Mrs Erlynne remains condemned for exactly the same fault. For all her heroic sacrifice, Mrs Erlynne is given only the dubious reward of a marriage to Lord Augustus. At the same time, Wilde refuses to stereotype the 'fallen' woman as the repentant sinner. Mrs Erlynne recognizes and sets aside the feelings of a parent – 'a heart doesn't suit me, Windermere. Somehow it doesn't go with modern dress'. This inversion of the conventions of Society Drama allows Wilde to expose, but not to disturb, the moral assumptions embedded in it. Darlington is dispatched abroad to work off his illicit and anti-social passion where it can do no harm. And Mrs Erlynne, while she can enjoy her aristocratic match, also has to live abroad. Her goodness might be apparent to Lady Windermere and to the audience, but it is not allowed to threaten the stability of London Society. Wilde's ending is comic in that his characters are all allowed a second chance to make amends for past mistakes; it is also satiric in the sense that it inverts the theatrical conventions with which he was working; but it is far from optimistic.

The ambiguous but none the less comic ending of the play is important because it reminds us of the conventions of the late nineteenth-century stage. Wilde (and Alexander) could mock the values of the audience who supported them, but that mockery had limits. Neither could ever afford the kind of social criticism to be found in the work of Henrik Ibsen or George Bernard Shaw. It is worth remembering that despite his sympathy with radical political views and with the non-profit-making avant-garde theatre clubs of the

[29] ibid., 163.

1890s (where Ibsen's and Shaw's early work was staged for very small audiences), Wilde craved approbation from those 'best circles' which his plays gently mocked. After all, he had spent the best part of twelve years (since leaving Oxford) trying to be taken seriously by that élite group which Max Beerbohm called the 'upper ten thousand'. It is also worth remembering that as long as those 'best circles' survived as a potent force in British society, Wilde's plays had an audience. Alexander's revivals of *Lady Windermere's Fan* in 1904 and 1911 were very successful. However those revivals had required costumes, furniture and topical allusions to be updated in order that Edwardian audiences could recognize themselves in the play rather than their late Victorian predecessors.

This need to update the plays, felt as early as four years after Wilde's death, reminds us of the subtlety and intimacy of his relationship to the subject and audience of the Society Comedies. The plays appeared much more dated after the upheavals brought about by the Great War had weakened the position of British social élites. That insecurity derived in part from a growing discrepancy between middle-class and aristocratic (or upper-middle-class) power and aspirations. In the 1890s there had been a much stronger continuity of values between these two social groups, so that middle-class audiences of the West-End theatres in the late nineteenth century could identify with the values represented on the stage. More precisely, the insecurity of the upper-middle classes allowed them to identify with Wilde's satire on the philistinism of lower-middle class values (particularly those of the professional world of bankers, stockbrokers, lawyers, solicitors and the clergy). By 1920, of course, the relative power and status of these groups had changed significantly, and so too had the role and identity of British middle-class society. Theatre audiences of the 1920s no longer necessarily shared the values and aspirations of the characters represented in Wilde's plays. As Joel H. Kaplan has pointed out, by this time it had become very difficult to recapture that sense of contemporaneity where the audience could identify in some sense with what was being enacted on the stage. Put more simply, modern-dress productions of a play such as *Lady Windermere's Fan* had become virtually impossible: 'Victorian manners in post-war garb created anachronisms too glaring to overlook', Kaplan comments.[30] A sense of anachronism distanced the audience from the stage; more importantly, it disabled the ways in which the play had operated as satire.

Since the 1920s, then, modern directors have had to find innovative ways of staging the play in order to recuperate its original

---

[30] Joel H. Kaplan, 'Wilde on the stage', in *The Cambridge Companion to Oscar Wilde*, ed. Peter Raby (1997), 249–75 (p. 260).

political edge. One interesting if unusual presentation was Ernst Lubitsch's 1925 silent film of the play. As Kaplan observes, by cutting the text Lubitsch could use the language of contemporary Hollywood cinema to evoke a materialism and opulence analogous to the 1890s West End, but relevant and specific to the consumerism of the 1920s. Of course for the theatre, this kind of reinterpretation, where linguistic effects are translated into visual equivalents, is not easy. The most recent productions of *Lady Windermere's Fan* have concentrated on radical reinterpretations of the text – on reading for what modern literary critics have called the play's subtexts. Invariably this reading has involved locating a subversive sexual politics submerged beneath the polite world of 1890s London Society. More precisely the heterosexual jealousies and insecurities in the play, which centre on issues of adultery and what constitutes a wise marriage, are reinterpreted in terms of the values of homosexual and homosocial societies. So most 1890s audiences saw the exclusive world of the male club and its attitudes to women (in Act III) as something quite innocuous and humorous. That scene takes on entirely different connotations when that exclusive male world is explicitly coded in terms of homosexual camaraderie. Similarly the consistent criticism of marriage and the *mores* of heterosexual behaviour become pointed when they are aligned directly with the male world of the dandy. Here it is worth reiterating a point made earlier, that Lord Darlington ceases to be an interesting and critical character once he 'comes out' as the heterosexual suitor of Lady Windermere.

The legitimation of these sorts of interpretations is of course one established by new accounts of Wilde's life, which is now impossible to read in terms other than that of the gay icon and the gay martyr. As a consequence, it is equally impossible for modern theatre-goers to see his plays free from the freight which has accrued from a century of speculating about his iconoclastic life and fetishizing his sexuality; we should not be surprised if modern directors have exploited the possibilities in juxtaposing the life and the work. At the same time, we should exercise caution in seeing Wilde in the 1890s in the light of the Wilde of the 1990s. We cannot assume that the radical politics which modern directors and readers find in the play were ever 'intended' by Wilde or available for his contemporary audience. Wilde the subversive writer, who uses but overturns the heterosexual morality of his time, is very much a modern creation: it is one that has been taken seriously only in the last twenty years. Moreover, it is possible to construct the 'subversive' Wilde only by a counter-intuitive reading of the plays – that is, by looking for hidden subtextual or coded meanings. Of course, no simple appeal to evidence can gainsay what is allegedly invisible or hidden (which would have to be explicit to be controverted). Hence it is difficult to disprove these subtextual interpretations.[31] However, we should remember that drama is a performance art. We can be certain that contemporary audiences would not have continued to patronize a play which offended them. The proper distinction to make, then, is not about the existence or otherwise of hidden codes, but the functions which the play possesses within particular cultures at particular moments in time: seen in these terms, Wilde's play continues to work for audiences, even if it requires reinterpretation.

The Play and its Drafts

It is now generally acknowledged that Wilde was a frequent and conscientious reviser of his work. Evidence for Wilde's actual writing practices, however, is rather uneven. More manuscripts and typescript drafts for the four Society Comedies survive than for the earlier works. There are manuscripts for only some of the poems, fewer still for the short stories, and virtually none for Wilde's journalism. One reason for this state of affairs is the bankruptcy proceedings brought against Wilde by the Marquess of Queensberry in 1895, which resulted in the dispersal of much of Wilde's literary property, including his manuscripts and typescripts. A more important reason exists in the collaborative nature of dramatic authorship, where many playwrights were open to suggestions made by the cast and the actor-manager (the end of the second act of *Lady Windermere's Fan* being a case in point). Rehearsal and part copies, which were kept together by the company and which part the modern editor can use to construct a history of a play's evolution, ensure that we have abundant evidence about the way Wilde set about learning the art of playwrighting. The changes made to the work which began life as manuscript notes entitled *A Good Woman* and which was published as *Lady Windermere's Fan* by the Bodley Head in 1893 shows how steep that learning curve was.

There are six surviving drafts and one unauthorized edition of *Lady Windermere's Fan*. Most of these differ markedly from each other and all differ significantly from the text that Wilde finally chose to print in 1893. They can be tentatively divided into three groups, each of which represents a major stage in the composition

---

[31] Recently Joseph Bristow has cautioned modern readers from assuming that Wilde would have understood himself in terms of the categories derived from modern gay theories; he has also reminded us of recent 'painstaking discussion [by historians] of how a category such as "homosexuality" came into being in the first place, and why it might not readily apply to the life and works of Wilde'. Joseph Bristow, ' "A complex multiform creature": Wilde's sexual identities', in *The Cambridge Companion to Oscar Wilde*, ed. Peter Raby (1997), 195–218 (p. 196).

of the final text. The first group comprises the manuscript draft at the British Library (BL) and a typescript under the earlier title of 'A Good Woman' at the William Andrews Clark Memorial Library in UCLA (C1). The second group comprises early acting versions. It includes a version in manuscript (not Wilde's), also at the Clark Library (Cms), and an acting version in typescript, again at the Clark (C2: this text has two separately typed copies of Acts II, III, and IV, but only one of Act I). The C2 typescripts are very similar and it is possible that one was a duplicate of the other. Also in this group we can include the text published in Britain as *Lady Windermere's Fan* (n.d.) by Samuel French (F). The text of this edition is different from every other surviving acting version or published edition of the play, and appears to be based on an earlier (and perhaps pirated) acting version as it has more textual features in common with C2 and Cms than with either the first edition or with the other acting copies. The third group includes a performance text (revised in manuscript by several hands) in the possession of the University of Texas (T) and the Licensing Copy (LC) – the only one dated, for it bears the receipt-stamp of the Lord Chamberlain's Office for 15 February 1892 (i.e. five days before the first performance). Once again these texts have many elements in common which set them apart from the other drafts.

The various redraftings and revisions of the play reveal certain features which can be used to illustrate its genesis. These include additional characters and changes in characterization and to the play's structure. But they also reveal that Wilde's conception of the play's central theme changed fundamentally during the course of revisions. Although a distinct pattern may be discerned in the revisions to the plot and to the development of the play's comic moments, a reason for this pattern is not easily found. Moreover, the exact revisions which Wilde made to the play are very complex in nature. The order of revision is not a simple chronological progression – that of draft A being revised to draft B, then to draft C and so on. Lines and speeches (and occasionally parts of scenes and act-endings) are discarded from earlier drafts only to be reincorporated into later ones. Each draft of the play gives evidence of Wilde working tentatively but often haphazardly to the final printed edition.

Although it contains some features which Wilde discarded for the later acting versions and revived for the first edition, the BL manuscript draft is markedly different from the other drafts of the play. There are only five characters, including a Lord Robert Erskine (a surname which Wilde had already used in 1889 in 'The Portrait of Mr W. H.'); Mrs Erlynne is Mrs Alwynne and Parker is Barker. The play begins with the entry of Lord Darlington, a character only sketchily drawn and who is more forward in his suggestion of adultery. He is without any of elements of the dandy which distinguish his character in the later drafts. Only some speeches are attributed to characters. The draft has little verbal polish and some of the scenes and characters of the later drafts are absent (such as some of the ballroom scenes of Act II and the characters of Graham, Hopper, Dumby, Lady Agatha and Lady Plymdale). While it has little of the wit of the later versions, the basic features of the plot are in place, but it presents its subject, the irresistible nature of adultery, much more forcefully. There is no indication of Mrs Erlynne's relationship with Lady Windermere until the final act.

By the time the C1 typed draft was complete, the play was much more fully settled in Wilde's mind. The opening exchange between Parker and Lady Windermere is in place, and Lord Darlington is much more fully characterized. Lady Windermere is forthright in her allegations about Mrs Erlynne, who in this draft is an unsophisticated blackmailer. Lord Augustus is more fully drawn and the part of Lady Agatha now has more lines (more in fact than in the first edition). The sequence of scenes in Act II is much altered and contains an additional lengthy altercation between Lord and Lady Windermere. Act IV is much longer and contains a scene where Lady Windermere tries to find a miniature of Mrs Erlynne, who is again revealed as a mother only in this act. The character of Hopper is not yet invented and an additional theme, that of the enduring quality of parental love, emerges.

In the absence of dates, it is difficult to assign to the second group of drafts an order of composition from internal features alone. Structure and characterization is much the same as in the first edition, although the drafts contain between 328 (C2) and 591 (F) substantive differences from it. Hopper is present for the first time, and the comic functions of Lord Augustus are now firmly established. The minor characters, however, are different from the first edition, as are the conclusions of Acts I and II. The obsessively adulterous nature of London Society is still the major theme.

T and LC together represent the closest surviving approximation to the text of the first performance; they do, however, differ from each other. The notion of the fundamental similarity of the 'good' and 'bad' woman is now much more firmly at the play's centre. Both drafts are very different from the first edition.

In 1893, twenty-one months after it was first performed, the first edition of the play (1st ed.) was published by Elkin Mathews and John Lane at the Bodley Head, a firm which had in the early 1890s established itself as a significant literary and dramatic publisher; the firm's list included works by Matthew Arnold, Edward Burne Jones, Sir Frederick (later Lord) Leighton, Christina Rossetti, William Michael Rossetti and John Ruskin. Wilde, however, was one of the Bodley Head's most prized authors – *Salomé* was to be their single most profitable book and *The Sphinx* their most expensive. The contract between publisher and writer reflects this prestige:

it specified an edition of 500 small-paper and 50 large-paper copies at the respective prices of 7s. 6d. and 15s. net. The books were elaborately produced collectors' items and had gold embossed designs by Charles Shannon. Wilde once more thoroughly revised his text for publication, and it is clear that he returned to earlier drafts for lines (and, indeed, whole speeches) which he had deleted from the second and third group of drafts. As a consequence, the published play is longer and has more characters than any of the drafts. Wilde's revisions from the final acting versions to the first edition are of three kinds. First, there are revisions to the play's structure. One of these was his decision to incorporate Alexander's advice (which is discussed above) by revealing the identity of Mrs Erlynne in Act II; another was the use of more characters (without speaking parts), also in Act II. (Of course, introducing a non-speaking character into a book is a far easier undertaking than hiring an actor for a non-speaking part on the stage.) Secondly, there are a large number of small but important stylistic revisions: the reinstatement of single words (especially adverbs) which change an emphasis or nuance of meaning, and the use of emphatic repetitions not present in the drafts. The third group of revisions concerns the lengthening (at times the doubling) of certain speeches. In general, speeches in the first edition are more melodramatically impassioned and more deliberately rhetorical than in any of the drafts.

Note on the Text and Textual and Critical Annotation

The text printed in this edition follows that of the Elkin Mathews and John Lane (Bodley Head) first edition of the play published in 1893. There is no reason to suppose that the changes incorporated into this edition were not made by Wilde or without his authority. It is clear that this text is in places profoundly different from what we know the text of the first performance must have been. While the case for reproducing a performance text has some force, arguments for reproducing the printed text are stronger, for Wilde had abundant opportunity to consider, and then accept or reject, the changes which were made to the play during rehearsal and its relatively long run. The annotation in the present volume notes the significant differences between the first edition and the nearest surviving approximations of the first performance (T and LC). It also notes what Wilde discarded from the two earliest drafts of the play (BL and C1) and subsequently reintroduced into the first edition. The revisions noted give some indication of Wilde's fidelity to his original conception and of the development of his knowledge of stagecraft. Occasionally, however, I have included what I judge to be a significant revision which appeared in a draft other than those noted above.

Critical annotation of the text has generally been restricted to explaining references or nuances of meaning which a contemporary audience would have readily caught but which are now lost to most readers. Where necessary I have compared Wilde's representation of the etiquette of London Society with two anonymous but popular handbooks of contemporary etiquette: *Manners and Rules of Good Society* (1888) and *The Habits of Good Society* (1890).

The punctuation of stage directions has been normalized to accord with New Mermaid practice. The spelling of words ending in *-ise* and some hyphenated words (for example, 'any-one', 'to-night', 'wide-spread') has been changed to accord with modern practice. Two errors of punctuation in the first edition have been silently emended.[32]

Note on the Staging

George Alexander's prompt-book for *Lady Windermere's Fan* has not survived. Without the specific information which he would have recorded in it, it is not possible to reconstruct accurately the first staging of the play. However, as both the general principles that informed Alexander's productions and many details about the St James's Theatre are known, it is possible to give a broad outline of the way in which Wilde's play would have been produced in 1892.

The St James's was a small theatre. It had been built in 1843; when it was altered in 1879 it could accommodate an audience of 1,200. The next major alterations took place between 1889 and 1890, the year in which Alexander took over the lease. Alexander himself had the auditorium redecorated, refurnished and electric lighting installed. In keeping with the size of the auditorium, the stage too was small (measuring 26 feet by 42 feet to 60 feet.[33] Alexander's productions reflected the intimate atmosphere of his theatre, for they featured convincingly realistic stage effects. As the plays he produced mirrored the manners and morals of the St James's audience, so his costumes, sets and stage properties exactly reproduced a physical environment with which they also would have been familiar. The realism of Alexander's sets and the meticulous attention he paid to the details of properties and costumes were celebrated at the time.[34] So although the stage directions which

---

[32] The following emendations have been made to the first edition: II, 488: '*Thanks!*' for '*Thanks?*' (the emended form occurs most frequently in the drafts); IV, 325: '*night.*' for '*night?*'

[33] See Diana Howard, *London Theatres and Music Halls 1850–1950* (1970).

[34] For a general account of the relationship between theatrical fashions and public taste, see Joel H. Kaplan and Sheila Stowell, *Theatre and Fashion: Oscar Wilde to the Suffragettes* (1994).

Wilde included in the 1893 Mathews and Lane edition of *Lady Windermere's Fan* differ considerably from the directions found in the acting editions, the precise detail which Wilde specifies almost certainly derives from Alexander's influence and practice.[35]

In the stage directions 'Left' and 'Right' indicate positions on stage as seen by the actors, not the audience.

[35] For details, see W. Macqueen Pope, *St James's: Theatre of Distinction* (1958), and Mason, *Sir George Alexander and the St James's Theatre*.

FURTHER READING

Bibliography

Ian Fletcher and John Stokes, 'Oscar Wilde', in *Anglo-Irish Literature: A Review of Research*, ed. R. J. Finneran (New York, 1976)

'Stuart Mason' [C. S. Millard], *Bibliography of Oscar Wilde* (1908; repr., with an introduction by Timothy D'Arch Smith, 1967)

E. H. Mikhail, *Oscar Wilde: An Annotated Bibliography of Criticism* (1978)

Thomas A. Mikolyzk, *Oscar Wilde: An Annotated Bibliography* (1993)

Ian Small, *Oscar Wilde Revalued: An Essay on New Methods and Materials of Research* (Greensboro, N.C., 1993)

Ian Small, *Oscar Wilde: Recent Research* (Greensboro, N.C., 2000)

Biography

Davis Coakley, *The Importance of Being Irish* (Dublin, 1994)

Richard Ellmann, *Oscar Wilde* (1987)

Rupert Hart-Davis, ed., *The Letters of Oscar Wilde* (1962; 1963)

Merlin Holland, *The Wilde Album* (1997)

Merlin Holland and Rupert Hart-Davies, eds., *The Complete Letters of Oscar Wilde* (2000)

H. Montgomery Hyde, *The Trials of Oscar Wilde* (1948; repr. New York, 1975)

E. H. Mikhail, ed., *Oscar Wilde, Interviews and Recollections* (2 vols., 1979)

Richard Pine, *Oscar Wilde* (Dublin, 1983)

Horst Schroeder, *Additions and Corrections to Richard Ellmann's 'Oscar Wilde'* (privately printed, Braunschweig, 1989)

Collections of Criticism

Karl Beckson, ed., *Oscar Wilde: The Critical Heritage* (1970)

Richard Ellmann, ed., *Oscar Wilde: A Collection of Critical Essays* (Englewood Cliffs, N.J., 1969; repr. 1986)

Regenia Gagnier, ed., *Critical Essays on Oscar Wilde* (New York, 1991)

Joel H. Kaplan, ed., *Modern Drama: Special Issue on Wilde*, 34 (1994)

Peter Raby, ed., *The Cambridge Companion to Oscar Wilde* (Cambridge, 1997)

George C. Sandelescu, ed., *Rediscovering Oscar Wilde*, Princess Grace Library Series 8 (Gerrard's Cross, 1994)

William Tydeman, *Wilde: Comedies: A Casebook* (1982)

Criticism
Karl Beckson, *The Oscar Wilde Encyclopedia* (New York, 1998)
Alan Bird, *The Plays of Oscar Wilde* (1977)
Jonathan Dollimore, *Sexual Dissidence: Augustine to Wilde, Freud to Foucault* (Oxford, 1991)
Regenia Gagnier, *The Idylls of the Marketplace: Oscar Wilde and the Victorian Public* (Stanford, 1987)
Arthur H. Ganz, 'The Divided Self in the Comedies of Oscar Wilde', *Modern Drama*, 3 (1960), 16–23
Ian Gregor, 'Comedy and Oscar Wilde', *Sewanee Review*, 74 (1966), 501–21
Josephine M. Guy and Ian Small, *Oscar Wilde's Profession: Writing and the Culture Industry in the late Nineteenth Century* (Oxford, 2000)
Joel H. Kaplan, ed., *Modern Drama* (Special Wilde number), 12, 1 (1994)
Joel H. Kaplan and Sheila Stowell, *Theatre and Fashion: Oscar Wilde to the Suffragettes* (Cambridge, 1994)
Norbert Kohl, *Oscar Wilde: The Works of a Conformist Rebel* (Cambridge, 1988)
Jerusha McCormack, 'Masks Without Faces: The Personalities of Oscar Wilde', *English Literature in Transition*, 22 (1979), 253–69
Christopher Nassaar, *Into the Demon Universe: A Literary Exploration of Oscar Wilde* (New Haven, Conn., 1974)
Kerry Powell, *Oscar Wilde and the Theatre of the 1890s* (Cambridge, 1990)
Peter Raby, *Oscar Wilde* (Cambridge, 1988)
Alan Sinfield, *The Wilde Century: Effeminacy, Oscar Wilde and the Queer Movement* (New York, 1994)
Rodney Shewan, *Art and Egotism* (1977)
John Stokes, *Oscar Wilde: Myths, Miracles and Imitations* (Cambridge, 1996)

LADY WINDERMERE'S FAN

A Play About
A Good Woman

By
OSCAR WILDE

To

The dear Memory

of

ROBERT EARL OF LYTTON

In Affection

and

Admiration

Dedication Edward Robert Bulwer, first Earl of Lytton (1831–91) and the son of Bulwer Lytton. Wilde and he 'had become during the last year [of Lytton's life] very great friends' (*Letters*, 299). Lytton was British Ambassador in Paris from 1887 until his death in November 1891 (when Wilde was revising and rewriting the play).

THE PERSONS OF THE PLAY
[St James's Theatre, 20 February 1892]

LORD WINDERMERE	*Mr George Alexander*
LORD DARLINGTON	*Mr Nutcombe Gould*
LORD AUGUSTUS LORTON	*Mr H. H. Vincent*
MR CECIL GRAHAM	*Mr Ben. Webster*
MR DUMBY	*Mr Vane-Tempest*
MR HOPPER	*Mr Alfred Holles*
PARKER (*Butler*)	*Mr V. Sansbury*
LADY WINDERMERE	*Miss Lily Hanbury*
THE DUCHESS OF BERWICK	*Miss Fanny Coleman*
LADY AGATHA CARLISLE	*Miss Laura Graves*
LADY PLYMDALE	*Miss Granville*
LADY JEDBURGH	*Miss B. Page*
LADY STUTFIELD	*Miss Madge Girdlestone*
MRS COWPER-COWPER	*Miss A. De Winton*
MRS ERLYNNE	*Miss Marion Terry*
ROSALIE (*Maid*)	*Miss Winifred Dolan*

The Persons of the Play from the 1st ed.
The names of Darlington and Windermere are present from the play's earliest forms and follow a pattern, frequent in Wilde, of appropriating place names for names of characters. Mrs Erlynne is Mrs Evlynne in early drafts and Lord Augustus Lorton is Lord Augustus Makham in BL. The names and number of the minor characters underwent considerable changes during the play's genesis. There were no Windermeres in the British peerage in the 1890s. The other titles did exist or had existed, but were no longer used, either because they were second or subsequent titles or because they were extinct. (The Darlington title, for example, became extinct in August 1891.)

THE SCENES OF THE PLAY

Act I   *Morning-room in Lord Windermere's house*
Act II   *Drawing-room in Lord Windermere's house*
Act III   *Lord Darlington's rooms*
Act IV   *Same as Act I*

Time—The Present
Place—London

The action of the play takes place within twenty-four hours, beginning on a Tuesday afternoon at five o'clock, and ending the next day at 1.30 p.m.

LADY WINDERMERE'S FAN

Act I

Scene: Morning-room of LORD WINDERMERE's *house in Carlton House Terrace. Doors C. and R. Bureau with books and papers R. Sofa with small tea-table L. Window opening on to terrace L. Table R.* LADY WINDERMERE *is at table R., arranging roses in a blue bowl*

Enter PARKER

PARKER
Is your ladyship at home this afternoon?
LADY WINDERMERE
Yes—who has called?
PARKER
Lord Darlington, my lady.

---

1 s.d. In the acting drafts of the play, these are much more detailed. They all mention specifically Lady Windermere's fan placed on a table. All that is retained here is the address, and addresses are usually important in Wilde's plays as they signify fine nuances of social discrimination. This address places the play politically and socially: close to prestigious clubs, Carlton House Terrace contained the residences of distinguished diplomats and statesmen. A late 19th-century audience would identify it with high diplomatic circles (Palmerston, for example, had lived there).

1 *at home* the question anticipates the tension between Lord D and Lady W later in the scene. The term indicated willingness to receive calls by visitors. Calls were made between 3 and 6 o'clock in the afternoon. The time of the call varied with the degree of intimacy of the visitor: little-known acquaintances from 3 to 4; better-known acquaintances from 4 to 5; close friends from 5 to 6—the hour of Lord D's visit. Calls by men on their own were rare. Parker's question intimates that he knows of some coldness in Lady W's attitude:

> If a servant is not sure as to whether his mistress wishes to see visitors or not, it is almost a direct offence to the . . . [caller] if he hesitates as to his answer, and leaves [him] . . . standing in the hall, while 'He will see if his mistress is "at home," ' perhaps returning with the unsatisfactory answer that she is 'Not at home'; in which case the intimation is . . . received as a personal exclusion'. (*Manners and Rules*, 41).

Servants would usually announce other visitors without further enquiry. Lady W is therefore *clearly* insisting that her interview with Lord D is *not* private.

LADY WINDERMERE (*Hesitates for a moment*)
Show him up—and I'm at home to anyone who calls.

PARKER
Yes, my lady.   *Exit C.*   5

LADY WINDERMERE
It's best for me to see him before tonight. I'm glad he's
come.

Enter PARKER *C.*

PARKER
Lord Darlington.

Enter LORD DARLINGTON *C. Exit* PARKER

LORD DARLINGTON
How do you do, Lady Windermere?

LADY WINDERMERE
How do you do, Lord Darlington? No, I can't shake hands   10
with you. My hands are all wet with these roses. Aren't
they lovely? They came up from Selby this morning.

LORD DARLINGTON
They are quite perfect. (*Sees a fan lying on the table*) And
what a wonderful fan! May I look at it?

LADY WINDERMERE
Do. Pretty, isn't it! It's got my name on it, and everything.   15
I have only just seen it myself. It's my husband's birthday
present to me. You know today is my birthday?

10 *shake hands* the greeting was quite usual in late 19th-century Society and not so
   formal as it might now seem. However, Lady W's reply suggests that Lord D
   has offered *his* hand first—once more suggesting (in terms of late 19th-century
   manners) undue forwardness on Lord D's part, for 'a man has no right to take a
   lady's hand until it is offered' (*Habits*, 287).

12 *Selby* Selby is mentioned three times during the play—here, and in Act IV. It
   is clearly intended to be the Windermeres' country estate. More specifically the
   emphasis on the rural aspects of Selby invokes the idea of a pastoral retreat
   from the moral complexity of the city. Actually the town of Selby had no estate
   of the size intended here by Wilde, although the famous abbey was owned by
   the Petre family. (Its restoration in 1871–73 by G. Gilbert Scott and 1889–90
   by J. Oldrid Scott made the town topical.) Wilde presumably chose Selby to
   indicate distance (both physical and metaphorical) from London, but the
   detail is very plausible. The Great Northern, the fastest railway in the world in
   1889, advertised expresses from King's Cross to Selby in a little over 3 hours:
   hence Lord W's suggestion that he and Lady W catch the 3.40 (IV, 48) is quite
   feasible. Dorian Gray's country estate is Selby Royal.

12 *this morning* only in 1st ed.

13 *quite* only in 1st ed. and C1.

LORD DARLINGTON
  No? Is it really?
LADY WINDERMERE
  Yes, I'm of age today. Quite an important day in my life,
  isn't it? That is why I am giving this party tonight. Do sit   20
  down.   *Still arranging flowers*
LORD DARLINGTON (*Sitting down*)
  I wish I had known it was your birthday, Lady Winder-
  mere. I would have covered the whole street in front of
  your house with flowers for you to walk on. They are made
  for you.   *A short pause*   25
LADY WINDERMERE
  Lord Darlington, you annoyed me last night at the Foreign
  Office. I am afraid you are going to annoy me again.
LORD DARLINGTON
  I, Lady Windermere?

Enter PARKER *and* FOOTMAN *C., with tray and tea things*

LADY WINDERMERE
  Put it there, Parker. That will do. (*Wipes her hands with her
  pocket-handkerchief, goes to tea-table L., and sits down*)
  Won't you come over, Lord Darlington?   30
                                               Exit PARKER *C.*
LORD DARLINGTON (*Takes chair and goes across L.C.*)
  I am quite miserable, Lady Windermere. You must tell me
  what I did.   *Sits down at table L.*
LADY WINDERMERE
  Well, you kept paying me elaborate compliments the
  whole evening.
LORD DARLINGTON (*Smiling*)
  Ah, nowadays we are all of us so hard up, that the only   35
  pleasant things to pay *are* compliments. They're the only
  things we *can* pay.
LADY WINDERMERE (*Shaking her head*)
  No, I am talking very seriously. You mustn't laugh, I am
  quite serious. I don't like compliments, and I don't see
  why a man should think he is pleasing a woman enorm-   40

19 *of age* i.e., twenty-one, an age specified in the early drafts of the play. At the
   time of the play's composition there was intense public debate about married
   women's rights—particularly property rights.
26-7 *the Foreign Office* entertainments at official institutions (in a semi-private
   capacity) formed part of the London Season (and hence the organization of
   those institutions was synchronized with it, as were the church and parlia-
   mentary calendars and the university year).

ously when he says to her a whole heap of things that he
doesn't mean.

LORD DARLINGTON

Ah, but I did mean them. *Takes tea which she offers him*

LADY WINDERMERE (*Gravely*)

I hope not. I should be sorry to have to quarrel with you,
Lord Darlington. I like you very much, you know that.   45
But I shouldn't like you at all if I thought you were what
most other men are. Believe me, you are better than most
other men, and I sometimes think you pretend to be worse.

LORD DARLINGTON

We all have our little vanities, Lady Windermere.

LADY WINDERMERE

Why do you make that your special one?   50

Still seated at table L.

LORD DARLINGTON (*Still seated L.C.*)

Oh, nowadays so many conceited people go about Society
pretending to be good, that I think it shows rather a sweet
and modest disposition to pretend to be bad. Besides,
there is this to be said. If you pretend to be good, the world
takes you very seriously. If you pretend to be bad, it   55
doesn't. Such is the astounding stupidity of optimism.

LADY WINDERMERE

Don't you *want* the world to take you seriously then, Lord
Darlington?

LORD DARLINGTON

No, not the world. Who are the people the world takes
seriously? All the dull people one can think of, from the   60
Bishops down to the bores. I should like *you* to take me
very seriously, Lady Windermere, *you* more than anyone
else in life.

LADY WINDERMERE

Why—why me?

LORD DARLINGTON (*After a slight hesitation*)

Because I think we might be great friends. Let us be great   65
friends. You may want a friend some day.

46–7 *what most other men are* announces a theme familiar in Society Drama, that of
the innate propensity of men to sexual immorality and hence of the necessity of
a dual standard of sexual ethics. cf. Lady Windermere below: 'Are *all* men
bad?' (I, 289).

55–6 *it doesn't* only in 1st ed.; in all drafts 'they don't'.

56 *astounding* only in 1st ed.

60–1 *from the Bishops . . . bores* only in 1st ed.

LADY WINDERMERE
  Why do you say that?
LORD DARLINGTON
  Oh!—we all want friends at times.
LADY WINDERMERE
  I think we're very good friends already, Lord Darlington.
  We can always remain so as long as you don't—   70
LORD DARLINGTON
  Don't what?
LADY WINDERMERE

Proud to be a Puritan.

  Don't spoil it by saying extravagant silly things to me. You
  think I am a Puritan, I suppose? Well, I have something of
  the Puritan in me. I was brought up like that. I am glad of
  it. My mother died when I was a mere child. I lived always   75
  with Lady Julia, my father's elder sister you know. She
  was stern to me, but she taught me, what the world is
  forgetting, the difference that there is between what is
  right and what is wrong. *She* allowed of no compromise. *I*
  allow of none.   80
LORD DARLINGTON
  My dear Lady Windermere!
LADY WINDERMERE (*Leaning back on the sofa*)
  You look on me as being behind the age.—Well, I am! I
  should be sorry to be on the same level as an age like this.
LORD DARLINGTON
  You think the age very bad?
LADY WINDERMERE

rival values of life.

  Yes. Nowadays people seem to look on life as a specula-   85
  tion. It is not a speculation. It is a sacrament. Its ideal is
  Love. Its purification is sacrifice.
LORD DARLINGTON (*Smiling*)
  Oh, anything is better than being sacrificed!   *— life's for living!*
LADY WINDERMERE (*Leaning forward*)
  Don't say that.

76 *Lady Julia* only in 1st ed. and C1; 'my aunt' in early drafts.
82 *behind the age* modernity was a topical issue in the 1880s and 1890s, not only
   among the artistic avant-garde but in Society as well. But to be abreast of the
   times (and fashions of conduct as well as of dress) involved also the implication
   of immorality.
86 *speculation* the eligibility of men and women depended heavily, although not
   exclusively, on their property; hence the metaphor from financial capitalism.
   Sufficient wealth could compensate for the lack of family connections (cf. the
   Duchess of B's attitude to Hopper). Lady W later pointedly asserts: 'Windermere and I married for love' (I, 293).

LORD DARLINGTON

   I do say it. I feel it—I know it.   90

Enter PARKER *C.*

PARKER

   The men want to know if they are to put the carpets on the
terrace for tonight, my lady?

LADY WINDERMERE

   You don't think it will rain, Lord Darlington, do you?

LORD DARLINGTON

   I won't hear of its raining on your birthday!

LADY WINDERMERE

   Tell them to do it at once, Parker.   *Exit* PARKER *C.*   95

LORD DARLINGTON (*Still seated*)

   Do you think then—of course I am only putting an imaginary instance—do you think that in the case of a young
married couple, say about two years married, if the husband suddenly becomes the intimate friend of a woman
of—well, more than doubtful character, is always calling   100
upon her, lunching with her, and probably paying her
bills—do you think that the wife should not console herself?

LADY WINDERMERE (*Frowning*)

   Console herself?

LORD DARLINGTON

   Yes, I think she should—I think she has the right.   105

LADY WINDERMERE

   Because the husband is vile—should the wife be vile also?

LORD DARLINGTON

   Vileness is a terrible word, Lady Windermere.

LADY WINDERMERE

   It is a terrible thing, Lord Darlington.

LORD DARLINGTON

   Do you know I am afraid that good people do a great deal of
harm in this world. Certainly the greatest harm they do is   110

100–2 *doubtful character* . . . *paying her bills* Lord D is of course alluding to Mrs E.
The implication is that she is a kept mistress.

106 *should the wife be vile also?* on the idea of woman paying back the man in kind,
see Jones's *The Case of Rebellious Susan* (Criterion, 1894), I, particularly:

> **LADY DARBY**
> Mr Harabin may have been indiscreet . . . and infatuated . . . and led
> away!
> **LADY SUSAN**
>
> Very well. I'm going to be indiscreet, and infatuated, and the rest of it.

that they make badness of such extraordinary importance.
It is absurd to divide people into good and bad. People are
either charming or tedious. I take the side of the charming,
and you, Lady Windermere, can't help belonging to them.

LADY WINDERMERE

Now, Lord Darlington. (*Rising and crossing R., front of* 115
him) Don't stir, I am merely going to finish my flowers.
                                        Goes to table R.C.

LORD DARLINGTON (*Rising and moving chair*)

And I must say I think you are very hard on modern life,
Lady Windermere. Of course there is much against it, I
admit. <u>Most women, for instance, nowadays, are rather
mercenary.</u>   120

LADY WINDERMERE

Don't talk about such people.

LORD DARLINGTON

Well then, setting mercenary people aside, who, of course,
are dreadful, do you think seriously that women who have
committed what the word calls a fault should never be
forgiven?   125

LADY WINDERMERE (*Standing at table*)

I think they should never be forgiven.

LORD DARLINGTON

And men? Do you think that there should be the same laws
for men as there are for women?

LADY WINDERMERE

Certainly!

LORD DARLINGTON

I think life too complex a thing to be settled by these hard 130
and fast rules.

LADY WINDERMERE

If we had 'these hard and fast rules', we should find life
much more simple.

---

112 *good and bad* ironically precisely Lady W's revised view in Act IV. Lord D's
avowal of attitudes the play finally endorses illustrates the ambivalence of the
portrayal of both characters.

127 *same laws* cf *A Woman of No Importance*, II:

    HESTER

    Don't have one law for men and another for women.
    You are unjust to women in England.

                    (*A Woman of No Importance*, 72 (*CW*, 450))

LORD DARLINGTON
  You allow of no exceptions?

LADY WINDERMERE
  None!   135

LORD DARLINGTON
  Ah, what a fascinating Puritan you are, Lady Windermere!

LADY WINDERMERE
  The adjective was unnecessary, Lord Darlington.   *— paradox*

LORD DARLINGTON
  I couldn't help it. I can resist everything except temptation.   140

LADY WINDERMERE
  You have the modern affectation of weakness.

LORD DARLINGTON (*Looking at her*)
  It's only an affectation, Lady Windermere.

                    Enter PARKER *C.*

PARKER
  The Duchess of Berwick and Lady Agatha Carlisle. *✦*

Enter the DUCHESS OF BERWICK *and* LADY AGATHA CARLISLE *C.*
                    Exit PARKER *C.*

134 *no exceptions* it is significant that Lord D's usual role as the spokesman for
    'advanced' opinions has been reversed and Lady W given views on the equality
    of the sexes that were much more radical than those generally held; here in fact
    Lady W is expressing Wilde's own views on equality.

138 *The adjective* in all drafts this speech also has the sentence 'You've forgotten
    your promise'.

139–40 *I can resist . . . temptation* perhaps the most famous paradox of the play; it
    recurs in slightly different forms in the other plays. cf. *A Woman Of No
    Importance*, III:

    KELVIL
      The secret of life is to resist temptation, Lady Stutfield.
    LORD ILLINGWORTH
      . . . Life's aim, if it has one, is simply to be always looking for tempta-
      tions. There are not nearly enough. I sometimes pass a whole day without
      coming across a single one.

                    (*A Woman of No Importance*, 126 (*CW*, 464))

143–6 *Duchess . . . Darlington* Wilde's application of titles is strictly accurate. So
    'an English duchess should be addressed as "Duchess" by all persons convers-
    ing with her belonging to the upper classes, and as "Your Grace" by all other
    classes' (*Manners and Rules*, 54). In the matter of introductions, sex always
    took precedence over rank, and so the Duchess of B introduces Lord D *to* her
    daughter, albeit very casually.

DUCHESS OF BERWICK (*Coming down C., and shaking hands*)
Dear Margaret, I am so pleased to see you. You remember
Agatha, don't you? (*Crossing L.C.*) How do you do, Lord   145
Darlington? I won't let you know my daughter, you are far
too wicked.

LORD DARLINGTON
Don't say that, Duchess. As a wicked man I am a complete
failure. Why, there are lots of people who say I have never
really done anything wrong in the whole course of my life.   150
Of course they only say it behind my back.

DUCHESS OF BERWICK
Isn't he dreadful? Agatha, this is Lord Darlington. Mind
you don't believe a word he says. (LORD DARLINGTON
crosses R.C.) No, no tea, thank you, dear. (*Crosses and sits
on sofa*) We have just had tea at Lady Markby's. Such bad   155
tea, too. It was quite undrinkable. I wasn't at all surprised.
Her own son-in-law supplies it. Agatha is looking forward
so much to your ball tonight, dear Margaret.

LADY WINDERMERE (*Seated L.C.*)
Oh, you mustn't think it is going to be a ball, Duchess. It is
only a dance in honour of my birthday. A small and early.   160

LORD DARLINGTON (*Standing L.C.*)
Very small, very early, and very select, Duchess.

---

157 *son-in-law* the implication is that the son-in-law is in trade and therefore of little
or no social significance. See *A Woman Of No Importance*, I:

> LADY CAROLINE
> . . . In my young days, Miss Worsley, one never met any one in society
> who worked for their living.
>
> (*A Woman of No Importance*, 4 (*CW*, 432))

Ironically the Duchess changes her attitude when it comes to her own son-in-
law to be (the son of a canned food merchant).

159 *ball* towards the end of the century private functions became more exclusive as
Society became more numerous. The difference between a ball and a dance is
therefore a significant one: 'at a dance the number of the guests varies from
eighty to two hundred; at a ball . . . from two hundred to five hundred'
(*Manners and Rules*, 88). Earlier authorities made the distinction at about 100
guests. The scale of entertaining also varied. The irony of the following lines is
clear. Balls existed in the main to introduce girls (like Agatha) to eligible
partners, who duly signed the girl's card. Balls were *not* for introducing the
(ineligible) Mrs Erlynnes of the 1890s into Society.

159–60 *It is only a dance* LC adds 'a small dance'.

160 *early* i.e., will finish early. The polite time for guests to depart was midnight;
the more fashionable time between 2.00 and 3.00 a.m. Lady W's modesty and
decorum is being emphasized.

DUCHESS OF BERWICK (*On sofa L.*)

Of course it's going to be select. But we know *that*, dear
Margaret, about *your* house. It is really one of the few
houses in London where I can take Agatha, and where I
feel perfectly secure about dear Berwick. I don't know   165
what society is coming to. The most dreadful people seem
to go everywhere. They certainly come to my parties—the
men get quite furious if one doesn't ask them. Really,
someone should make a stand against it.

LADY WINDERMERE

I will, Duchess. I will have no one in my house about   170
whom there is any scandal.

LORD DARLINGTON (*R.C.*)

Oh, don't say that, Lady Windermere. I should never be
admitted!   *Sitting*

DUCHESS OF BERWICK

Oh, men don't matter. With women it is different. We're
good. Some of us are, at least. But we are positively getting   175
elbowed into the corner. Our husbands would really forget
our existence if we didn't nag at them from time to time,
just to remind them that we have a perfect legal right to do
so.

LORD DARLINGTON

It's a curious thing, Duchess, about the game of mar-   180
riage—a game, by the way, that is going out of fashion—the
wives hold all the honours, and invariably lose the odd
trick.

DUCHESS OF BERWICK

The odd trick? Is that the husband, Lord Darlington?

LORD DARLINGTON

It would be rather a good name for the modern husband.   185

DUCHESS OF BERWICK

Dear Lord Darlington, how thoroughly depraved you are!

LADY WINDERMERE

Lord Darlington is trivial.

LORD DARLINGTON

Ah, don't say that, Lady Windermere.

163–4 *one of the few houses* the Duchess of B is expressing what was a widely held
    fear. As more people were deemed eligible for acceptance into Society, so it
    became increasingly difficult to know in person everyone taking part in the
    London Season.
182–3 *the odd trick* the reference is to whist or the early varieties of bridge (which
    had been invented in 1886). To lose the 'odd' trick is to lose by six tricks to
    seven.

LADY WINDERMERE
  Why do you *talk* so trivially about life, then?

LORD DARLINGTON
  Because I think that life is far too important a thing ever to   190
  talk seriously about it.   *Moves up C.*

DUCHESS OF BERWICK
  What does he mean? Do, as a concession to my poor wits,
  Lord Darlington, just explain to me what you really mean.

LORD DARLINGTON (*Coming down back of table*)
  I think I had better not, Duchess. Nowadays to be intelli-
  gible is to be found out. Goodbye! (*Shakes hands with*   195
  DUCHESS) And now—(*Goes up stage*) Lady Windermere,
  goodbye. I may come tonight, mayn't I? Do let me come.

LADY WINDERMERE (*Standing up stage with* LORD DARLING-
  TON)
  Yes, certainly. But you are not to say foolish, insincere
  things to people.

LORD DARLINGTON (*Smiling*)
  Ah! you are beginning to reform me. It is a dangerous   200
  thing to reform anyone, Lady Windermere.
                                      Bows, and exit C.

DUCHESS OF BERWICK (*Who has risen, goes C.*)
  What a charming, wicked creature! I like him so much.
  I'm quite delighted he's gone! How sweet you're looking!
  Where *do* you get your gowns? And now I must tell you
  how sorry I am for you, dear Margaret. (*Crosses to sofa and*   205
  sits with LADY WINDERMERE) Agatha darling!

LADY AGATHA
  Yes, mamma.   *Rises*

DUCHESS OF BERWICK
  Will you go and look over the photograph album that I see
  there?

LADY AGATHA
  Yes, mamma.   *Goes to table up L.*   210

DUCHESS OF BERWICK
  Dear girl! She is so fond of photographs of Switzerland.

190–1 *life is . . . to talk seriously about it* a favourite paradox. cf. *A Woman Of No Importance*, I:

> LORD ILLINGWORTH
>   Taking sides is the beginning of sincerity, and earnestness follows shortly
>   afterwards, and the human being becomes a bore.
>   (*A Woman Of No Importance*, 21 (*CW*, 437))

197 *Do let me come* only in 1st ed.
204 *Where* do *you get your gowns?* only in 1st ed.

Such a pure taste, I think. But I really am so sorry for you, Margaret.

LADY WINDERMERE (*Smiling*)

Why, Duchess?

DUCHESS OF BERWICK

Oh, on account of that horrid woman. She dresses so well,   215
too, which makes it much worse, sets such a dreadful
example. Augustus—you know my disreputable
brother—such a trial to us all—well, Augustus is completely infatuated about her. It is quite scandalous, for she
is absolutely inadmissible into society. Many a woman has   220
a past, but I am told that she has at least a dozen, and that
they all fit.

LADY WINDERMERE

Whom are you talking about, Duchess?

DUCHESS OF BERWICK

About Mrs Erlynne.

LADY WINDERMERE

Mrs Erlynne? I never heard of her, Duchess. And what *has*   225
she to do with me?

DUCHESS OF BERWICK

My poor child! Agatha, darling!

LADY AGATHA

Yes, mamma.

DUCHESS OF BERWICK

Will you go out on the terrace and look at the sunset?

LADY AGATHA

Yes, mamma.   *Exit through window L.*   230

212–13 *sorry for you, Margaret* Cms, C1, F, have 'sorry for you, dear'.
220–2 *Many a woman . . . they all fit* Mrs E's past should, of course, have been with
  a Mr E. Hence Lady W's question below:

'Is there a Mr Erlynne—or is he a myth?' (I, 388)

'Mrs' invariably indicated to theatre audiences a woman who had compromised
herself. But Wilde is making light of these expectations. cf. below:

LORD AUGUSTUS

I prefer women with a past. They're always so demmed amusing to talk to.
(III, 247–8)

and cf. *An Ideal Husband*, II:

SIR ROBERT CHILTERN

. . . She looks like a woman with a past, doesn't she?

LORD GORING

Most pretty women do.

(*An Ideal Husband*, 92 (*CW*, 509))

DUCHESS OF BERWICK

Sweet girl! So devoted to sunsets! Shows such refinement of feeling, does it not? After all, there is nothing like Nature, is there?

LADY WINDERMERE

But what is it, Duchess? Why do you talk to me about this person?   235

DUCHESS OF BERWICK

Don't you really know? I assure you we're all so distressed about it. Only last night at dear Lady Jansen's everyone was saying how extraordinary it was that, of all men in London, Windermere should behave in such a way.

LADY WINDERMERE

My husband—what has *he* got to do with any woman of   240
that kind?

DUCHESS OF BERWICK

Ah, what indeed, dear? That is the point. He goes to see her continually, and stops for hours at a time, and while he is there she is not at home to anyone. Not that many ladies call on her, dear, but she has a great many disreputable   245
men friends—my own brother particularly, as I told you—and that is what makes it so dreadful about Winder-mere. We looked upon *him* as being such a model husband, but I am afraid there is no doubt about it. My dear nieces—you know the Saville girls, don't you?—such nice   250
domestic creatures—plain, dreadfully plain, but so good—well, they're always at the window doing fancy work, and making ugly things for the poor, which I think so useful of them in these dreadful socialistic days, and this

---

231–3 *devoted to Sunsets . . . Nature, is there?* the primacy of the natural world as a moral agent was familiar in 19th-century culture from Wordsworth to Ruskin. It was a belief that writers who were associated with Aestheticism, particularly Wilde, questioned increasingly. cf. 'The Decay Of Lying': 'Nature, no less than life, is an imitation of Art' (*Intentions*, 41 (*CW*, 984)). Wilde is using 'refinement' in a double sense: the notion of the 'socially correct' with an allusion (perhaps ironic) to the Paterian notion of the cultivation of sensibility.

251–2 *plain . . . so good* the relationship between morality and physical unattrac-tiveness is a constant theme in the plays. cf III, 274, where Graham comments: 'a woman who moralizes is invariably plain'; and *An Ideal Husband*, III:

LORD GORING

But women who have common-sense are so curiously plain, father, aren't they?

(*An Ideal Husband*, 156 (*CW*, 527))

terrible woman has taken a house in Curzon Street, right   255
opposite them—such a respectable street, too. I don't
know what we're coming to! And they tell me that Windermere goes there four and five times a week—they *see*
him. They can't help it—and although they never talk
scandal, they—well, of course—they remark on it to   260
everyone. And the worst of it all is that I have been told
that this woman has got a great deal of money out of
somebody, for it seems that she came to London six
months ago without anything at all to speak of, and now
she has this charming house in Mayfair, drives her ponies   265
in the Park every afternoon and all—well, all—since she
has known poor dear Windermere.

LADY WINDERMERE
Oh, I can't believe it!

DUCHESS OF BERWICK
But it's quite true, my dear. The whole of London knows
it. That is why I felt it was better to come and talk to you,   270
and advise you to take Windermere away at once to Homburg or to Aix, where he'll have something to amuse him,
and where you can watch him all day long. I assure you,
my dear, that on several occasions after I was first married,
I had to pretend to be very ill, and was obliged to drink the   275
most unpleasant mineral waters, merely to get Berwick out
of town. He was so extremely susceptible. Though I am

---

255 *Curzon Street* in Mayfair, and so a respectable address: the detail places Mrs
Erlynne as a parvenu. BL makes the point more emphatically when Lady W
later says: 'I didn't know people of that kind lived in our part of town. I thought
they lived north of the Park'—i.e., Bayswater, a recent speculative development.

266 *Park* i.e., Hyde Park. 'From 3 to 6.30 are the received hours for the afternoon
drive during the summer, and from 2.30 to 4.30 during the winter. . . . A
married lady can, as a matter of course, drive unaccompanied' (*Manners and
Rules*, 203–4).

266–7 *since she has known* another suggestion that Mrs E is Lord W's (kept)
mistress.

271 *away at once* C1 and T add 'not to the country—men get so bored there, if they
are not firing their horrid guns off'.

271 *Homburg* in July 1892, Wilde himself took the waters at Homburg. It was in the
1890s a favourite spa of the English aristocracy and Royalty.

275–6 *drink . . . waters* a continental spa is being alluded to. The usual way of
removal from Society and possible embarrassment was to go abroad. So Lord
A and Mrs E decide to live 'out of England' in IV, 413.

277 *extremely* added to 1st ed.

bound to say he never gave away any large sums of money
to anybody. He is far too high-principled for that!

LADY WINDERMERE (*Interrupting*)

Duchess, Duchess, it's impossible! (*Rising and crossing*   280
stage to C.) We are only married two years. Our child is but
six months old.   *Sits in chair R. of L. table*

DUCHESS OF BERWICK

Ah, the dear pretty baby! How is the little darling? Is it a
boy or a girl? I hope a girl—Ah, no, I remember it's a boy!
I'm so sorry. Boys are so wicked. My boy is excessively   285
immoral. You wouldn't believe at what hours he comes
home. And he's only left Oxford a few months—I really
don't know what they teach them there.

LADY WINDERMERE

Are *all* men bad?

DUCHESS OF BERWICK

Oh, all of them, my dear, all of them, without any excep-   290
tion. And they never grow any better. Men become old,
but they never become good.

LADY WINDERMERE

Windermere and I married for love.

DUCHESS OF BERWICK

Yes, we begin like that. It was only Berwick's brutal and
incessant threats of suicide that made me accept him at all,   295
and before the year was out, he was running after all kinds
of petticoats, every colour, every shape, every material. In
fact, before the honeymoon was over, I caught him wink-
ing at my maid, a most pretty, respectable girl. I dismissed

285 *Boys are so wicked* the Duchess's relish in proclaiming the proclivities of brother
and son further illustrates the dual standard towards sexual behaviour in men
and women.

287 *Oxford a few months* i.e., that he has only recently finished his education and
that he has thus achieved full age. But Wilde is being ironic. In the late 1870s
and 1880s Oxford was the cradle of the Aesthetic Movement and was thus
associated with the charges of moral decadence that that movement attracted.
cf. the ironic reference in *The Importance of Being Earnest*, III, 221:

LADY BRACKNELL
Untruthful! My nephew Algernon? Impossible! He is an Oxonian.
(*CW*, 375).

There is perhaps a private joke in these references to Oxford. By the early 1890s
Wilde was visiting Oxford to solicit undergraduates.

289 *Are all men bad?* this picks up a central theme of Society Drama: that the
different moral codes of men and women are the consequences of different
emotional and physical constitutions. See Introduction.

her at once without a character.—No, I remember I passed   300
her on to my sister; poor dear Sir George is so short-
sighted, I thought it wouldn't matter. But it did,
though—it was most unfortunate. (*Rises*) And now, my
dear child, I must go, as we are dining out. And mind you
don't take this little aberration of Windermere's too much   305
to heart. Just take him abroad, and he'll come back to you
all right.

LADY WINDERMERE
Come back to me?   *C.*

DUCHESS OF BERWICK (*L.C.*)
Yes, dear, these wicked women get our husbands away
from us, but they always come back, slightly damaged, of   310
course. And don't make scenes, men hate them!

LADY WINDERMERE
It is very kind of you, Duchess, to come and tell me all this.
But I can't believe that my husband is untrue to me.

DUCHESS OF BERWICK
Pretty child! I was like that once. Now I know that all men
are monsters. (LADY WINDERMERE *rings bell*) The only   315
thing to do is to feed the wretches well. A good cook does
wonders, and that I know you have. My dear Margaret,
you are not going to cry?

LADY WINDERMERE
You needn't be afraid, Duchess, I never cry.

DUCHESS OF BERWICK
That's quite right, dear. Crying is the refuge of plain   320
women but the ruin of pretty ones. Agatha, darling!

LADY AGATHA (*Entering L.*)
Yes, mamma.   *Stands back of table L.C.*

---

304 *dining out* T adds 'and I know it will take me two hours to get into my new dress.
    It seems to me that the dresses get tighter and tighter every year. Have you
    remarked that?' (C1 is substantially the same.) The Duchess's comments were
    correct for fashionable dress in the early 1890s (a 19-inch waist was the
    ambition of the fashionable). It is interesting that Wilde discarded the joke in
    the 1st ed.

306 *Just take him abroad* the Duchess of B reiterates the common theatrical advice to
    the victim of adultery; it involved forgiveness conditional upon a trip abroad
    (i.e., temporary removal from Society).

311 *men hate them* BL, C1, and T in slightly differing forms add: 'No, tomorrow
    tell Windermere's valet to pack up his master's things and to carry the wretch
    off to Homburg'.

316 *wretches* only in 1st ed., in other versions 'brutes'. Another example of
    Wilde's stylistically precise revision for the 1st ed.

DUCHESS OF BERWICK

Come and bid goodbye to Lady Windermere, and thank
her for your charming visit. (*Coming down again*) And by
the way, I must thank you for sending a card to Mr   325
Hopper—he's that rich young Australian people are taking
such notice of just at present. His father made a great
fortune by selling some kind of food in circular tins—most
palatable, I believe—I fancy it is the thing the servants
always refuse to eat. But the son is quite interesting. I   330
think he's attracted by dear Agatha's clever talk. Of course,
we should be very sorry to lose her, but I think that a
mother who doesn't part with a daughter every season has
no real affection. We're coming tonight, dear. (PARKER
opens C. doors) And remember my advice, take the poor   335
fellow out of town at once, it is the only thing to do.
Goodbye, once more; come, Agatha.

Exeunt DUCHESS and LADY AGATHA C.

LADY WINDERMERE

How horrible! I understand now what Lord Darlington
meant by the imaginary instance of the couple not two
years married. Oh! it can't be true—she spoke of enormous   340
sums of money paid to this woman. I know where Arthur
keeps his bank book—in one of the drawers of that desk. I
might find out by that. I *will* find out. (*Opens drawer*) No,
it is some hideous mistake. (*Rises and goes C.*) Some silly
scandal! He loves *me*! He loves *me*! But why should I not   345
look? I am his wife, I have a right to look! (*Returns to
bureau, takes out book and examines it, page by page, smiles
and gives a sigh of relief*) I knew it! there is not a word of
truth in this stupid story. (*Puts book back in drawer. As she
does so, starts and takes out another book*) A second
book—private—locked! (*Tries to open it, but fails. Sees   350
paper knife on bureau, and with it cuts cover from book. Begins*

---

325 *a card* see as well below (Mrs Erlynne's invitation). 'The invitation card is the
      usual "at home" card, the word "Dancing" being printed in the corner of the
      card' (*Manners and Rules*, 96). Invitations were issued in the name of the
      hostess only, hence Lord W's request that Lady W invite Mrs E (below). It was
      quite normal for a lady to ask for an invitation for a friend or acquaint-
      ance—although rarely with the transparency of the Duchess of B's motives.

334 *real affection* F, T, Cms, C2, and LC add (in slightly differing forms) 'or no real
      brains, which is worse'.

335–6 *take the poor fellow . . . do* not in LC.

337 *Goodbye* T, F, and LC have: 'Come, Agatha; goodbye again till tonight'
      following this.   350 s.d. *paper knife* C1 and T: 'Moorish paper knife'.

to start at the first page) 'Mrs Erlynne—£600—Mrs Erlynne—£700—Mrs Erlynne—£400'. Oh! it is true! it is true! How horrible!   *Throws book on floor*

Enter LORD WINDERMERE *C.*

LORD WINDERMERE

Well, dear, has the fan been sent home yet? (*Going R.C. Sees book*) Margaret, you have cut open my bank book.   355
You have no right to do such a thing!

LADY WINDERMERE

You think it wrong that you are found out, don't you?

LORD WINDERMERE

I think it wrong that a wife should spy on her husband.

LADY WINDERMERE

I did not spy on you. I never knew of this woman's existence till half an hour ago. Someone who pitied me was kind   360
enough to tell me what everyone in London knows
already—your daily visits to Curzon Street, your mad
infatuation, the monstrous sums of money you squander
on this infamous woman!   *Crossing L.*

LORD WINDERMERE

Margaret! don't talk like that of Mrs Erlynne, you don't   365
know how unjust it is!

LADY WINDERMERE (*Turning to him*)

You are very jealous of Mrs Erlynne's honour. I wish you
had been as jealous of mine.

LORD WINDERMERE

Your honour is untouched, Margaret. You don't think for
a moment that—   *Puts book back into desk*   370

LADY WINDERMERE

I think that you spend your money strangely. That is all.
Oh, don't imagine I mind about the money. As far as I am·
concerned, you may squander everything we have. But
what I *do* mind is that you who have loved me, you who
have taught me to love you, should pass from the love that   375
is given to the love that is bought. Oh, it's horrible! (*Sits on*

356   *no right* the obvious and primary meaning is that Lady W has no *moral* right.
Ironically the line is literally true as well, for until recently a married woman's
property was her husband's.

356   *to do such a thing* T: 'to open my bureau, or to meddle into any of my private
affairs'. C1 is substantially the same.

371   *I think that you spend* BL has: 'I think that you go for your amours to an
expensive market'. C1 is similar.

376   *the love that is bought* making explicit the allusions made throughout the act that
Mrs E is being kept by Lord W.

sofa) And it is I who feel degraded! *you* don't feel anything.
I feel stained, utterly stained. You can't realize how hideous the last six months seem to me now—every kiss you
have given me is tainted in my memory.   380

LORD WINDERMERE (*Crossing to her*)

Don't say that, Margaret. I never loved anyone in the
whole world but you.

LADY WINDERMERE (*Rises*)

Who is this woman, then? Why do you take a house for
her?

LORD WINDERMERE

I did not take a house for her.   385

LADY WINDERMERE

You gave her the money to do it, which is the same thing.

LORD WINDERMERE

Margaret, as far as I have known Mrs Erlynne—

LADY WINDERMERE

Is there a Mr Erlynne—or is he a myth?

LORD WINDERMERE

Her husband died many years ago. She is alone in the
world.   390

LADY WINDERMERE

No relations?   *A pause*

LORD WINDERMERE

None.

LADY WINDERMERE

Rather curious, isn't it?   *L.*

LORD WINDERMERE (*L.C.*)

Margaret, I was saying to you—and I beg you to listen to

---

378 *utterly stained* only in 1st ed.

391–2 *No relations . . . None* only in 1st ed., C1, and BL (in a slightly different
form). Entrance to Society consisted partly in the establishing of the credentials of the whole family. (So, for example, a gentleman would be presented at
court by his prospective wife's most distinguished *male* relative.) The topic is
familiar in Society Drama. In Jones's *Mrs Dane's Defence* Miss Hindemarsh
personates the dead Mrs Dane in order to gain entry into Society. The whole of
that play is quasi-judicial examination of her credentials. Lord A makes the
same point: 'Demmed nuisance relations! But they make one so demmed
respectable'.Cf. also Lady Bracknell's interrogation of Jack in *The Importance of
Being Earnest*, especially I, 584–5:

> LADY BRACKNELL
>
> I would strongly advise you, Mr Worthing, to try and acquire some
> relations as soon as possible.

(*CW*, 334)

me—that as far as I have known Mrs Erlynne, she has   395
conducted herself well. If years ago—

LADY WINDERMERE

Oh! (*Crossing R.C.*) I don't want details about her life!

LORD WINDERMERE (*C.*)

I am not going to give you any details about her life. I tell
you simply this—Mrs Erlynne was once honoured, loved,
respected. She was well born, she had position—she lost   400
everything—threw it away, if you like. That makes it all
the more bitter. Misfortunes one can endure—they come
from outside, they are accidents. But to suffer for one's
own faults—ah!—there is the sting of life. It was twenty
years ago, too. She was little more than a girl then. She had   405
been a wife for even less time than you have.

LADY WINDERMERE

I am not interested in her—and—you should not mention
this woman and me in the same breath. It is an error of
taste.   *Sitting R. at desk*

LORD WINDERMERE

Margaret, you could save this woman. She wants to get   410
back into society, and she wants you to help her.

Crossing to her

LADY WINDERMERE

Me!

LORD WINDERMERE

Yes, you.

LADY WINDERMERE

How impertinent of her!   *A pause*

LORD WINDERMERE

Margaret, I came to ask you a great favour, and I still ask it   415
of you, though you have discovered what I had intended
you should never have known, that I have given Mrs
Erlynne a large sum of money. I want you to send her an
invitation for our party tonight.   *Standing L. of her*

LADY WINDERMERE

You are mad!   *Rises*   420

LORD WINDERMERE

I entreat you. People may chatter about her, do chatter
about her, of course, but they don't know anything definite
against her. She has been to several houses—not to houses
where you would go, I admit, but still to houses where
women who are in what is called Society nowadays do go.   425
That does not content her. She wants you to receive her
once.

LADY WINDERMERE

As a triumph for her, I suppose?

LORD WINDERMERE

No; but because she knows that you are a good
woman—and that if she comes here once she will have a　430
chance of a happier, a surer life than she has had. She will
make no further effort to know you. Won't you help a
woman who is trying to get back?

LADY WINDERMERE

No! If a woman really repents, she never wishes to return
to the society that has made or seen her ruin.　435

LORD WINDERMERE

I beg of you.

LADY WINDERMERE (*Crossing to door R.*)

I am going to dress for dinner, and don't mention the
subject again this evening. Arthur (*Going to him C.*), you
fancy because I have no father or mother that I am alone in
the world, and that you can treat me as you choose. You are　440
wrong, I have friends, many friends.

LORD WINDERMERE (*L.C.*)

Margaret, you are talking foolishly, recklessly. I won't
argue with you, but I insist upon your asking Mrs Erlynne
tonight.

LADY WINDERMERE (*R.C.*)

I shall do nothing of the kind.　　　　　　*Crossing L.C.*　445

LORD WINDERMERE

You refuse?　　　　　　　　　　　　　　　　*C.*

LADY WINDERMERE

Absolutely!

LORD WINDERMERE

Ah, Margaret, do this for my sake; it is her last chance.

LADY WINDERMERE

What has that to do with me?

LORD WINDERMERE

How hard good women are!　450

LADY WINDERMERE

How weak bad men are!

LORD WINDERMERE

Margaret, none of us men may be good enough for the
women we marry—that is quite true—but you don't
imagine I would ever—oh, the suggestion is monstrous!

LADY WINDERMERE

Why should *you* be different from other men? I am told　455

that there is hardly a husband in London who does not
waste his life over *some* shameful passion.

LORD WINDERMERE

I am not one of them.

LADY WINDERMERE

I am not sure of that!

LORD WINDERMERE

You are sure in your heart. But don't make chasm after   460
chasm between us. God knows the last few minutes have
thrust us wide enough apart. Sit down and write the card.

LADY WINDERMERE

Nothing in the whole world would induce me.

LORD WINDERMERE (*Crossing to bureau*)

Then I will!   *Rings electric bell, sits and writes card*

LADY WINDERMERE

You are going to invite this woman?   *Crossing to him*   465

LORD WINDERMERE

Yes.   *Pause*

Enter PARKER

Parker!

PARKER

Yes, my lord.   *Comes down L.C.*

LORD WINDERMERE

Have this note sent to Mrs Erlynne at No. 84A Curzon
Street. (*Crossing to L.C. and giving note to* PARKER) There is   470
no answer!   *Exit* PARKER *C.*

LADY WINDERMERE

Arthur, if that woman comes here, I shall insult her.

LORD WINDERMERE

Margaret, don't say that.

LADY WINDERMERE

I mean it.

LORD WINDERMERE

Child, if you did such a thing, there's not a woman in   475
London who wouldn't pity you.

LADY WINDERMERE

There is not a *good* woman in London who would not
applaud me. We have been too lax. We must make an
example. I propose to begin tonight. (*Picking up fan*) Yes,

469 *No. 84A* early drafts have different numbers (BL and C1: '12': T and LC:
'99'). There was no such number in 1892. It is clear that Wilde's first alteration
was intended to avoid any reference to a specific house.
473–4 *Margaret, don't say that . . . mean it* not in LC.

you gave me this fan today; it was your birthday present. If   480
that woman crosses my threshold, I shall strike her across
the face with it.

LORD WINDERMERE

Margaret, you couldn't do such a thing.

LADY WINDERMERE

You don't know me!   *Moves R.*

Enter PARKER

Parker!   485

PARKER

Yes, my lady.

LADY WINDERMERE

I shall dine in my own room. I don't want dinner, in fact.
See that everything is ready by half-past ten. And, Parker,
be sure you pronounce the names of the guests very dis-
tinctly tonight. Sometimes you speak so fast that I miss   490
them. I am particularly anxious to hear the names quite
clearly, so as to make no mistake. You understand, Parker?

PARKER

Yes, my lady.

LADY WINDERMERE

That will do! (*Exit* PARKER *C.*) (*Speaking to* LORD WINDER-
MERE) Arthur, if that woman comes here—I warn you—   495

LORD WINDERMERE

Margaret, you'll ruin us!

LADY WINDERMERE

Us! From this moment my life is separate from yours. But
if you wish to avoid a public scandal, write at once to this
woman, and tell her that I forbid her to come here!

LORD WINDERMERE

I will not—I cannot—she must come!   500

LADY WINDERMERE

Then I shall do exactly as I have said. (*Goes R.*) You leave
me no choice.   *Exit R.*

486 *Yes, my lady* after this line T has:

> LADY WINDERMERE
> And hand me that fan.
> [PARKER *goes to table, takes fan and gives it to* LADY W. LORD W *makes a gesture
> to stop him—then restrains himself.*]

C1, F, and LC are similar.

488 *half-past ten* the usual time for balls to begin.

LORD WINDERMERE (*Calling after her*)
Margaret! Margaret! (*A pause*) My God! What shall I do?
I dare not tell her who this woman really is. The shame
would kill her.   505
Sinks down into a chair and buries his face in his hands ✳

Act-Drop

Act II

Scene: Drawing-room in LORD WINDERMERE's *house. Door R.U.*
opening into ballroom, where band is playing. Door L. through
which guests are entering. Door L.U. opens on to illuminated
terrace. Palms, flowers, and brilliant lights. Room crowded with
guests. LADY WINDERMERE *is receiving them*

DUCHESS OF BERWICK (*Up C.*)
So strange Lord Windermere isn't here. Mr Hopper is very
late, too. You have kept those five dances for him, Agatha?
Comes down

LADY AGATHA
Yes, mamma.

503–5 *Margaret . . . kill her* one of the most famous revisions in the play. Alexander
wanted Mrs E's real identity revealed at this point (as did some critics
later)—and indeed such a revelation seems to have been at one point Wilde's
original intention. So C2, Cms, F (in slightly differing forms) have:

I daren't tell her that this woman is her own mother.

Both BL and C1 keep Mrs E's identity a secret until Act IV; so do T and LC,
which have only 'Margaret—My God! What shall I do?' As it is, the real
relationship between Mrs E and Lady W is strongly hinted at.

1 s.d. Lady Windermere's 'small and early' is much grander than the dance
envisaged in Act I.
All drafts except BL describe the room as follows: 'Style Louis Seize. White
walls. Red and gold furniture'. Moreover, a boudoir is specified as one of the
adjoining rooms in all these drafts.

DUCHESS OF BERWICK (*Sitting on sofa*)

    Just let me see your card. I'm so glad Lady Windermere
has revived cards.—They're a mother's only safeguard.   5
You dear simple little thing! (*Scratches out two names*) No
nice girl should ever waltz with such particularly younger
sons! It looks so fast! The last two dances you might pass
on the terrace with Mr Hopper.

Enter MR DUMBY *and* LADY PLYMDALE *from the ballroom*

LADY AGATHA

    Yes, mamma.   10

DUCHESS OF BERWICK (*Fanning herself*)

    The air is so pleasant there.

PARKER

    Mrs Cowper-Cowper. Lady Stutfield. Sir James Royston.
Mr Guy Berkeley.

These people enter as announced

DUMBY

    Good evening, Lady Stutfield. I suppose this will be the
last ball of the season?   15

LADY STUTFIELD

    I suppose so, Mr Dumby. It's been a delightful season,
hasn't it?

DUMBY

    Quite delightful! Good evening, Duchess. I suppose this
will be the last ball of the season?

4–5 *I'm so glad . . . safeguard* young ladies' cards allowed chaperones to scrutin-
ize dancing (and hence prospective or possible marriage) partners; hence the
Duchess of B's attitude to Lady Agatha is making explicit the reasons for
the more formal 'policing' of Society, for younger sons stood to inherit less than
the eldest. The irony of the speech is in the Duchess's automatic assumption of
the self-evident ineligibility of younger sons. Another indication of the slightly
'old-fashioned' morality of Lady W's house is the reference to the waltz, which
was declining in popularity as a *fashionable* dance in the last decades of the
century.

11 s.d. *Fanning herself* the stuffiness of ballrooms and the consequent inconveni-
ence for guests were a topic that exercised many writers of etiquette manuals.

12–13 *Mrs Cowper-Cowper . . . Berkeley* the number and names of these characters differ greatly in the early versions. In F, T, and LC there is no Lady
Stutfield, her speeches being given to Lady W in F and to Lady Jedburgh in T
and LC.

DUCHESS OF BERWICK

I suppose so, Mr Dumby. It has been a very dull season,   20
hasn't it?

DUMBY

Dreadfully dull! Dreadfully dull!

MRS COWPER-COWPER

Good evening, Mr Dumby. I suppose this will be the last
ball of the season?

DUMBY

Oh, I think not. There'll probably be two more.   25

Wanders back to LADY PLYMDALE

PARKER

Mr Rufford. Lady Jedburgh and Miss Graham. Mr Hopper.

These people enter as announced

HOPPER

How do you do, Lady Windermere? How do you do,
Duchess?   *Bows to* LADY AGATHA

DUCHESS OF BERWICK

Dear Mr Hopper, how nice of you to come so early. We all   30
know how you are run after in London.

HOPPER

Capital place, London! They are not nearly so exclusive in
London as they are in Sydney.

DUCHESS OF BERWICK

Ah! we know your value, Mr Hopper. We wish there were
more like you. It would make life so much easier. Do you   35
know, Mr Hopper, dear Agatha and I are so much
interested in Australia. It must be so pretty with all the
dear little kangaroos flying about. Agatha has found it on
the map. What a curious shape it is! Just like a large
packing case. However, it is a very young country, isn't it?   40

HOPPER

Wasn't it made at the same time as the others, Duchess?

26-7 *Mr Rufford . . . Mr Hopper* in F, T, and LC only Hopper is announced; in
Cms Hopper is announced in a separate speech, perhaps to indicate Wilde's
intention that he should be differentiated from the other guests—indicated too
by a ms addition to T: 'guests shd be announced before Hopper'.

31 *run after* F, T, Cms, C2, and LC: 'so run after'. Part of the point of the Duchess
of B's speech is that she takes over the role of welcoming H from the hostess.

32 *Capital* in all drafts 'Jolly'.

DUCHESS OF BERWICK
How clever you are, Mr Hopper. You have a cleverness quite of your own. Now I mustn't keep you.

HOPPER
But I should like to dance with Lady Agatha, Duchess.

DUCHESS OF BERWICK
Well, I *hope* she has a dance left. Have you a dance left,   45
Agatha?

LADY AGATHA
Yes, mamma.

DUCHESS OF BERWICK
The next one?

LADY AGATHA
Yes, mamma.

HOPPER
May I have the pleasure?   LADY AGATHA *bows*   50

DUCHESS OF BERWICK
Mind you take great care of my little chatterbox, Mr
Hopper. LADY AGATHA *and* MR HOPPER *pass into ballroom*

Enter LORD WINDERMERE *L.*

LORD WINDERMERE
Margaret, I want to speak to you.

LADY WINDERMERE
In a moment.   *The music stops*

PARKER
Lord Augustus Lorton.   55

Enter LORD AUGUSTUS

LORD AUGUSTUS
Good evening, Lady Windermere.

DUCHESS OF BERWICK
Sir James, will you take me into the ballroom? Augustus
has been dining with us tonight. I really have had quite
enough of dear Augustus for the moment.

SIR JAMES ROYSTON *gives the* DUCHESS *his arm and escorts her
into the ballroom*

---

54 *In a moment* T has a ms note: 'Lady W does not know Mrs E is coming, so does
not think she needs Lord Darlington's aid'. At this point in LC Parker
announces Lord D.

57 *Sir James* in early versions other characters are addressed; F: 'Lord Plimdale'
[*sic*]; T, Cms, and LC: 'Mr Dumby'.

PARKER

Mr and Mrs Arthur Bowden. Lord and Lady Paisley.   60
Lord Darlington.

These people enter as announced

LORD AUGUSTUS (*Coming up to* LORD WINDERMERE)

Want to speak to you particularly, dear boy. I'm worn to a
shadow. Know I don't look it. None of us men do look
what we really are. Demmed good thing, too. What I want
to know is this. Who is she? Where does she come from?   65
Why hasn't she got any demmed relations? Demmed nuisance, relations! But they make one so demmed respectable.

LORD WINDERMERE

You are talking of Mrs Erlynne, I suppose? I only met her
six months ago. Till then, I never knew of her existence.   70

LORD AUGUSTUS

You have seen a good deal of her since then.

LORD WINDERMERE (*Coldly*)

Yes, I have seen a good deal of her since then. I have just
seen her.

LORD AUGUSTUS

Egad! the women are very down on her. I have been dining
with Arabella this evening! By Jove! you should have   75
heard what she said about Mrs Erlynne. She didn't leave a
rag on her. . . . (*Aside*) Berwick and I told her that didn't
matter much, as the lady in question must have an
extremely fine figure. You should have seen Arabella's
expression! . . . But, look here, dear boy. I don't know   80
what to do about Mrs Erlynne. Egad! I might be married
to her; she treats me with such demmed indifference.

60–1 *Mr and Mrs Arthur Bowden . . . Darlington* this speech is not in LC.
64 *Demmed* the prolific use of 'damned' as a verbal mannerism for Lord A is only in
C1 in the early drafts. Consistently omitted from other drafts, and changed to
'demmed' in ms in T and incorporated into 1st ed. This use of specific stage
slang identifies Lord A as a man-about-town or a 'masher'.
81–2 *I might be . . . indifference* a familiar quip in the plays. cf., for example, *A
Woman Of No Importance*, II:

    LADY HUNSTANTON

       . . . I am told that, nowadays, all the married men live like bachelors,
      and all the bachelors like married men.

             (*A Woman Of No Importance*, 52 (*CW*, 444))
cf. also Lady P's paradox that indifference is a binding cement: 'women of that
kind . . . form the basis of other people's marriages' (II, 234–6).

She's deuced clever, too! She explains everything. Egad!
she explains you. She has got any amount of explanations
for you—and all of them different. 85

LORD WINDERMERE

No explanations are necessary about my friendship with
Mrs Erlynne.

LORD AUGUSTUS

Hem! Well, look here, dear old fellow. Do you think she
will ever get into this demmed thing called Society? Would
you introduce her to your wife? No use beating about the 90
confounded bush. Would you do that?

LORD WINDERMERE

Mrs Erlynne is coming here tonight.

LORD AUGUSTUS

Your wife has sent her a card?

LORD WINDERMERE

Mrs Erlynne has received a card.

LORD AUGUSTUS

Then she's all right, dear boy. But why didn't you tell me 95
that before. It would have saved me a heap of worry and
demmed misunderstandings!

LADY AGATHA *and* MR HOPPER *cross and exit on terrace L.U.E.*

PARKER

Mr Cecil Graham!

Enter MR CECIL GRAHAM

CECIL GRAHAM (*Bows to* LADY WINDERMERE, *passes over and
shakes hands with* LORD WINDERMERE)

Good evening, Arthur. Why don't you ask me how I am? I
like people to ask me how I am. It shows a widespread 100
interest in my health. Now, tonight I am not at all well.
Been dining with my people. Wonder why it is one's people
are always so tedious? My father would talk morality after

---

91 *confounded* only in 1st ed.

dinner. I told him he was old enough to know better. But
my experience is that as soon as people are old enough to   105
know better, they don't know anything at all. Hullo,
Tuppy! Hear you're going to be married again; thought
you were tired of that game.

LORD AUGUSTUS

You're excessively trivial, my dear boy, excessively trivial!

CECIL GRAHAM

By the way, Tuppy, which is it? Have you been twice   110
married and once divorced, or twice divorced and once
married? I say you've been twice divorced and once married. It seems so much more probable.

LORD AUGUSTUS

I have a very bad memory. I really don't remember which.

Moves away R.

LADY PLYMDALE

Lord Windermere, I've something most particular to ask   115
you.

LORD WINDERMERE

I am afraid—if you will excuse me—I must join my wife.

LADY PLYMDALE

Oh, you mustn't dream of such a thing. It's most dangerous nowadays for a husband to pay any attention to his wife
in public. It always makes people think that he beats her   120
when they're alone. The world has grown so suspicious of
anything that looks like a happy married life. But I'll tell
you what it is at supper.   *Moves towards door of ballroom*

104–6 *I told him . . . anything at all* another familiar paradox. Wilde habitually
    emphasized the merits of youth and frequently represented himself as being
    younger than he actually was. cf. *An Ideal Husband*, IV:
        LORD CAVERSHAM
        Why don't you try to do something useful in life?
        LORD GORING
        I am far too young.
        LORD CAVERSHAM (*testily*)
        I hate this affectation of youth, sir. It is a great deal too prevalent
        nowadays.
        LORD GORING
        Youth isn't an affectation. Youth is an art.
                                   (*An Ideal Husband*, 199 (*CW*, 539))
    cf. also *The Importance of Being Earnest*, I, 703–4:
        GWENDOLEN
        The old-fashioned respect for the young is fast dying out. (*CW*, 338)
115–23 *Lord Windermere . . . is at supper* a late revision which is only in 1st ed. and
    LC. In T Lady P's speech occurs just before Mrs E's entrance.

LORD WINDERMERE (*C.*)

Margaret! I *must* speak to you.

LADY WINDERMERE

Will you hold my fan for me, Lord Darlington? Thanks.   125
Comes down to him

LORD WINDERMERE (*Crossing to her*)

Margaret, what you said before dinner was, of course, impossible?

LADY WINDERMERE

That woman is not coming here tonight!

LORD WINDERMERE (*R.C.*)

Mrs Erlynne is coming here, and if you in any way annoy or wound her, you will bring shame and sorrow on us both.   130
Remember that! Ah, Margaret! only trust me! A wife should trust her husband!

LADY WINDERMERE (*C.*)

London is full of women who trust their husbands. One can always recognize them. They look so thoroughly unhappy. I am not going to be one of them. (*Moves up*)   135
Lord Darlington, will you give me back my fan, please? Thanks. . . . A useful thing a fan, isn't it? . . . I want a friend tonight, Lord Darlington: I didn't know I would want one so soon.

LORD DARLINGTON

Lady Windermere! I knew the time would come some day;   140
but why tonight?

LORD WINDERMERE

I *will* tell her. I must. It would be terrible if there were any scene. Margaret . . .

PARKER

Mrs Erlynne!

LORD WINDERMERE *starts.* MRS ERLYNNE *enters, very beautifully dressed and very dignified.* LADY WINDERMERE *clutches at her fan, then lets it drop on the floor. She bows coldly to* MRS

---

124 *I* must *speak to you* not in LC.
137 *A useful thing a fan, isn't it?* not in F, Cms, or C2. Cms and C2 have instead:
 'LORD W: I must tell her the truth. If anything were to happen here it would be terrible'. F has 'LORD W: I must tell her this woman is her own mother'. See Introduction.
142–8 *I* will *tell her . . . to come* the order and composition of these speeches underwent heavy revisions in all versions. See Appendix (*The Entrance of Mrs Erlynne*).

ERLYNNE, *who bows to her sweetly in turn, and sails into the room*

LORD DARLINGTON
   You have dropped your fan, Lady Windermere.   145
                              Picks it up and hands it to her
MRS ERLYNNE (*C.*)
   How do you do, again, Lord Windermere? How charming
   your sweet wife looks! Quite a picture!
LORD WINDERMERE (*In a low voice*)
   It was terribly rash of you to come!
MRS ERLYNNE (*Smiling*)
   The wisest thing I ever did in my life. And, by the way,
   you must pay me a good deal of attention this evening. I am   150
   afraid of the women. You must introduce me to some of
   them. The men I can always manage. How do you do,
   Lord Augustus? You have quite neglected me lately. I
   have not seen you since yesterday. I am afraid you're
   faithless. Everyone told me so.   155
LORD AUGUSTUS (*R.*)
   Now really, Mrs Erlynne, allow me to explain.
MRS ERLYNNE (*R.C.*)
   No, dear Lord Augustus, you can't explain anything. It is
   your chief charm.
LORD AUGUSTUS
   Ah! if you find charms in me, Mrs Erlynne—

They converse together. LORD WINDERMERE *moves uneasily about the room watching* MRS ERLYNNE

LORD DARLINGTON (*To* LADY WINDERMERE)
   How pale you are!   160
LADY WINDERMERE
   Cowards are always pale!
LORD DARLINGTON
   You look faint. Come out on the terrace.

162 *You look faint* only in 1st ed. and T where it is deleted in ms. This and previous
   two speeches underwent much revision in the drafts.

LADY WINDERMERE
  Yes. (*To* PARKER) Parker, send my cloak out.
MRS ERLYNNE (*Crossing to her*)
  Lady Windermere, how beautifully your terrace is illumi-
  nated. Reminds me of Prince Doria's at Rome. (LADY 165
  WINDERMERE *bows coldly, and goes off with* LORD DARLING-
  TON) Oh, how do you do, Mr Graham? Isn't that your
  aunt, Lady Jedburgh? I should so much like to know her.
CECIL GRAHAM (*After a moment's hesitation and embarrassment*)
  Oh, certainly, if you wish it. Aunt Caroline, allow me to
  introduce Mrs Erlynne.
MRS ERLYNNE
  So pleased to meet you, Lady Jedburgh. (*Sits beside her on* 170
  the sofa) Your nephew and I are great friends. I am so much
  interested in his political career. I think he's sure to be a
  wonderful success. He thinks like a Tory and talks like
  a Radical, and that's so important nowadays. He's such a
  brilliant talker, too. But we all know from whom he 175
  inherits that. Lord Allandale was saying to me only yesterday, in the Park, that Mr Graham talks almost as well as his
  aunt.
LADY JEDBURGH (*R.*)
  Most kind of you to say these charming things to me!
        MRS ERLYNNE *smiles, and continues conversation*
DUMBY (*To* CECIL GRAHAM)
  Did you introduce Mrs Erlynne to Lady Jedburgh? 180
CECIL GRAHAM
  Had to, my dear fellow. Couldn't help it! That woman can
  make one do anything she wants. How, I don't know.

---

165 *Doria's* in all early versions 'Dorian's'. After this speech, T has (deleted in ms)

> LORD D
>   I understand everything now.
> LADY W
>   Hush!

168 *Caroline* 'Emily' in early drafts.
168–9 *allow me to introduce Mrs Erlynne* Graham breaks the usual rules governing
  introduction by ignoring precedence, for the person of highest rank (here Lady
  Jedburgh) decides whether an introduction should take place; the correct
  order of introduction, however, *is* observed.
181–2 *That woman ... don't know* only in 1st ed.

DUMBY

Hope to goodness she won't speak to me!

Saunters towards LADY PLYMDALE

MRS ERLYNNE (*C. to* LADY JEDBURGH)

On Thursday? With great pleasure. (*Rises, and speaks to* LORD WINDERMERE, *laughing*) What a bore it is to have to be 185
civil to these old dowagers! But they always insist on it!

LADY PLYMDALE (*To* MR DUMBY)

Who is that well-dressed woman talking to Windermere?

DUMBY

Haven't got the slightest idea! Looks like an *édition de luxe* of a wicked French novel, meant specially for the English market.   190

MRS ERLYNNE

So that is poor Dumby with Lady Plymdale? I hear she is frightfully jealous of him. He doesn't seem anxious to speak to me tonight. I suppose he is afraid of her. Those straw-coloured women have dreadful tempers. Do you know, I think I'll dance with you first, Windermere. (LORD   195
WINDERMERE *bites his lip and frowns*) It will make Lord Augustus so jealous! Lord Augustus! (LORD AUGUSTUS *comes down*) Lord Windermere insists on my dancing with him first, and, as it's his own house, I can't well refuse. You know I would much sooner dance with you.   200

LORD AUGUSTUS (*With a low bow*)

I wish I could think so, Mrs Erlynne.

MRS ERLYNNE

You know it far too well. I can fancy a person dancing through life with you and finding it charming.

LORD AUGUSTUS (*Placing his hand on his white waistcoat*)

Oh, thank you, thank you. You are the most adorable of all ladies!   205

188–90 *édition de luxe . . . English market* in the last two decades of the century, the immoral influence of French fiction was a topical issue. In Vernon Lee's *Miss Brown*, for example, Edmund Lewis tries to proposition Anne Brown by giving her a copy of Gautier's *Mademoiselle de Maupin* and in Wilde's *The Picture of Dorian Gray* it is implied that Huysmans's *A Rebours* serves a similarly demoralizing purpose.

193 *I suppose he is afraid of her* LC has: 'Rather impertinent of him'.

193–5 *Those straw-coloured . . . I think* only in 1st ed. T has as a ms addition: 'It's quite brutal the way women behave nowadays to men who are not their husbands, isn't it?'

194–5 *Do you know* only in 1st ed.

202–3 *I can fancy . . . charming* here LC has: 'But you are to have the next, and the one after too, if you like.'

MRS ERLYNNE

What a nice speech! So simple and so sincere! Just the sort
of speech I like. Well, you shall hold my bouquet. (*Goes
towards ballroom on* LORD WINDERMERE's *arm*) Ah, Mr
Dumby, how are you? I am so sorry I have been out the last
three times you have called. Come and lunch on Friday.   210

DUMBY (*With perfect nonchalance*)

Delighted!

LADY PLYMDALE *glares with indignation at* MR DUMBY. LORD
AUGUSTUS *follows* MRS ERLYNNE *and* LORD WINDERMERE *into
the ballroom holding bouquet*

LADY PLYMDALE (*To* MR DUMBY)

What an absolute brute you are! I never can believe a word
you say! Why did you tell me you didn't know her? What
do you mean by calling on her three times running? You
are not to go to lunch there; of course you understand that?   215

DUMBY

My dear Laura, I wouldn't dream of going!

LADY PLYMDALE

You haven't told me her name yet! Who is she?

DUMBY (*Coughs slightly and smooths his hair*)

She's a Mrs Erlynne.

206–7 *Just the sort of speech I like* only in 1st ed.
210 *Friday* after this LC has:

> DUMBY
> I'm afraid I can't.
> MRS ERLYNNE
> Saturday—Sunday?
> DUMBY
> Delighted.
> LORD AUGUSTUS
> Dumby!

The effect of the revisions of this scene is to present Mrs Erlynne as a much less
mercenary and flirtatious figure.

216 *My dear Laura* only in 1st ed. T (in a ms revision) and C1 have: 'My dear child'.
Both forms emphasize the illicit (because adulterous) intimacy between the
two.

218 *She's a Mrs Erlynne* before this LC has:

> DUMBY
> I quite forget her name. How stupid of me.
> LADY PLIMDALE
> Tell me at once, or I shall leave the house.
> DUMBY
> If I do tell you, I think you *will* leave the house[.]

LADY PLYMDALE
  That woman!
DUMBY
  Yes; that is what everyone calls her.   220
LADY PLYMDALE
  How very interesting! How intensely interesting! I really
  must have a good stare at her. (*Goes to door of ballroom and
  looks in*) I have heard the most shocking things about her.
  They say she is ruining poor Windermere. And Lady
  Windermere, who goes in for being so proper, invites her!   225
  How extremely amusing! It takes a thoroughly good
  woman to do a thoroughly stupid thing. You are to lunch
  there on Friday!
DUMBY
  Why?
LADY PLYMDALE
  Because I want you to take my husband with you. He has   230
  been so attentive lately, that he has become a perfect
  nuisance. Now, this woman is just the thing for him. He'll
  dance attendance upon her as long as she lets him, and
  won't bother me. I assure you, women of that kind are
  most useful. They form the basis of other people's mar-   235
  riages.
DUMBY
  What a mystery you are!
LADY PLYMDALE (*Looking at him*)
  I wish *you* were!
DUMBY
  I am—to myself. I am the only person in the world I should
  like to know thoroughly; but I don't see any chance of it   240
  just at present.

They pass into the ballroom, and LADY WINDERMERE *and* LORD
DARLINGTON *enter from the terrace*

  220 *Yes; that is . . . calls her* only in 1st ed.
  224 *poor Windermere* after this sentence, C1 and T (deleted in ms) have: 'and she is
      absolutely unscrupulous'.
  226–7 *It takes . . . stupid thing* only in 1st ed.
  230 *my husband with you* at this point in LC Dumby says: 'I shall be delighted'.
  231 *so attentive* extending the recurrent joke on marital indifference, and both a foil
      to Lady W's sense of neglect and turning round Lord D's arguments for the
      legitimacy of taking 'consolation' when deserted.
  232 *thing for him* after this sentence T and LC have: 'He never parts with a penny,
      so she won't get anything out of him'.
  235–6 *They form the basis . . . marriages* not in LC.

LADY WINDERMERE

Yes. Her coming here is monstrous, unbearable. I know now what you meant today at tea time. Why didn't you tell me right out? You should have!

LORD DARLINGTON

I couldn't! A man can't tell these things about another   245
man! But if I had known he was going to make you ask her here tonight, I think I would have told you. That insult, at any rate, you would have been spared.

LADY WINDERMERE

I did not ask her. He insisted on her coming—against my entreaties—against my commands. Oh! the house is   250
tainted for me! I feel that every woman here sneers at me as she dances by with my husband. What have I done to deserve this? I gave him all my life. He took it—used it—spoiled it! I am degraded in my own eyes; and I lack courage—I am a coward!   *Sits down on sofa*   255

LORD DARLINGTON

If I know you at all, I know that you can't live with a man who treats you like this! What sort of life would you have with him? You would feel that he was lying to you every moment of the day. You would feel that the look in his eyes was false, his voice false, his touch false, his passion false.   260
He would come to you when he was weary of others; you would have to comfort him. He would come to you when he was devoted to others; you would have to charm him. You would have to be to him the mask of his real life, the cloak to hide his secret.   265

LADY WINDERMERE

You are right—you are terribly right. But where am I to turn? You said you would be my friend, Lord Darlington.—Tell me, what am I to do? Be my friend now.

LORD DARLINGTON

Between men and women there is no friendship possible.

---

242 *Her coming . . . unbearable* in F this sentence is given to Lord D. It is not in LC.

250–1 *Oh! the house . . . for me* only in 1st ed.

264–5 *the cloak . . . secret* only in 1st ed., BL, and C1. Wilde's revision emphasizes the significance of concealment in the play, for Lord W is already his wife's cloak to hide the secret of her relationship to Mrs E, just as Mrs E becomes the cloak to hide Lady W's secret and Lady W hides Mrs E's secret from Lord A.

266 *you are terribly right* only in 1st ed.

268 *Be my friend now* only in 1st ed.

There is passion, enmity, worship, love, but no friend-   270
ship. I love you—
LADY WINDERMERE
No, no!   *Rises*
LORD DARLINGTON
Yes, I love you! You are more to me than anything in the
whole world. What does your husband give you? Nothing.
Whatever is in him he gives to this wretched woman,   275
whom he has thrust into your society, into your home, to
shame you before everyone. I offer you my life—
LADY WINDERMERE
Lord Darlington!
LORD DARLINGTON
My life—my whole life. Take it, and do with it what you
will. . . . I love you—love you as I have never loved any   280
living thing. From the moment I met you I loved you,
loved you blindly, adoringly, madly! You did not know it
then—you know it now! Leave this house tonight. I won't
tell you that the world matters nothing, or the world's
voice, or the voice of society. They matter a great deal.   285
They matter far too much. But there are moments when
one has to choose between living one's own life, fully,
entirely, completely—or dragging out some false, shallow,
degrading existence that the world in its hypocrisy
demands. You have that moment now. Choose! Oh, my   290
love, choose!
LADY WINDERMERE (*Moving slowly away from him, and looking
at him with startled eyes*)
I have not the courage.
LORD DARLINGTON (*Following her*)
Yes; you have the courage. There may be six months of
pain, of disgrace even, but when you no longer bear his
name, when you bear mine, all will be well. Margaret, my   295
love, my wife that shall be some day—yes, my wife! You

273 *Yes, I love you* Lord D's declaration is of course the dramatic climax of the act,
       but the most important consequence in terms of the play's structure is that by
       becoming so deeply involved in breaking Society's sexual *mores*, he abandons
       the role of dandy, which now passes to Graham.
275–7 *Whatever is in him . . . before everyone* only in 1st ed.
289–90 *that the world . . . demands* only in 1st ed. and C1 (in a slightly different
       form).
290–1 *Oh, my love, choose!* only in 1st ed. and C1. The revisions to these speeches
       between Lord D and Lady W have the effect of making them more impassioned
       and more studiedly rhetorical.

know it! What are you now? This woman has the place that
belongs by right to you. Oh! go—go out of this house, with
head erect, with a smile upon your lips, with courage in
your eyes. All London will know why you did it; and who   300
will blame you? No one. If they do, what matter? Wrong?
What is wrong? It's wrong for a man to abandon his wife
for a shameless woman. It is wrong for a wife to remain
with a man who so dishonours her. You said once you
would make no compromise with things. Make none now.   305
Be brave! Be yourself!

LADY WINDERMERE

I am afraid of being myself. Let me think! Let me wait!
My husband may return to me.   *Sits down on sofa*

LORD DARLINGTON

And you would take him back! You are not what I thought
you were. You are just the same as every other woman.   310
You would stand anything rather than face the censure of a
world, whose praise you would despise. In a week you will
be driving with this woman in the Park. She will be your
constant guest—your dearest friend. You would endure
anything rather than break with one blow this monstrous   315
tie. You are right. You have no courage; none!

LADY WINDERMERE

Ah, give me time to think. I cannot answer you now.
                    Passes her hand nervously over her brow

LORD DARLINGTON

It must be now or not at all.

LADY WINDERMERE (*Rising from the sofa*)

Then, not at all!   *A pause*

LORD DARLINGTON

You break my heart!   320

LADY WINDERMERE

Mine is already broken.   *A pause*

LORD DARLINGTON

Tomorrow I leave England. This is the last time I shall
ever look on you. You will never see me again. For one
moment our lives met—our souls touched. They must
never meet or touch again. Goodbye, Margaret.   *Exit*   325

297–8 *the place that belongs by right to you* LC: 'your place'.
312 *you would despise* T: 'you affect to despise'. LC: 'you despise'.
312–16 *In a week . . . monstrous tie* only here and in C1, T, and (in a different,
      shorter form) LC.
323–5 *For one moment . . . touch again* not in Cms, C2, or LC; in C1 and a ms
      addition to T (in a slightly different form).

LADY WINDERMERE

How alone I am in life! How terribly alone!

The music stops. Enter the DUCHESS OF BERWICK *and* LORD
PAISLEY *laughing and talking. Other guests come on from
ballroom*

DUCHESS OF BERWICK

Dear Margaret, I've just been having such a delightful chat
with Mrs Erlynne. I am so sorry for what I said to you this
afternoon about her. Of course, she must be all right if *you*
invite her. A most attractive woman, and has such sensible   330
views on life. Told me she entirely disapproved of people
marrying more than once, so I feel quite safe about poor
Augustus. Can't imagine why people speak against her.
It's those horrid nieces of mine—the Saville girls—they're
always talking scandal. Still, I should go to Homburg,   335
dear, I really should. She is just a little too attractive. But
where is Agatha? Oh, there she is! (LADY AGATHA *and* MR
HOPPER *enter from terrace L.U.E.*) Mr Hopper, I am very,
very angry with you. You have taken Agatha out on the
terrace, and she is so delicate.   340

HOPPER (*L.C.*)

Awfully sorry, Duchess. We went out for a moment and
then got chatting together.

DUCHESS OF BERWICK (*C.*)

Ah, about dear Australia, I suppose?

HOPPER

Yes!

DUCHESS OF BERWICK

Agatha, darling!   *Beckons her over*   345

LADY AGATHA

Yes, mamma!

DUCHESS OF BERWICK (*Aside*)

Did Mr Hopper definitely—

LADY AGATHA

Yes, mamma.

DUCHESS OF BERWICK

And what answer did you give him, dear child?

327–8 *I've just been . . . with Mrs Erlynne* not in LC.

329 *must be all right* the light reversal of attitudes to Mrs E is an ironic parallel to the
    later volte-face in Lord and Lady W's attitudes.

330–3 *and has such . . . poor Augustus* only in 1st ed. (The whole speech is much
    changed in T.)

344 *Yes.* in T this speech is Lady A's.

LADY AGATHA

    Yes, mamma.   350

DUCHESS OF BERWICK (*Affectionately*)

    My dear one! You always say the right thing. Mr Hopper!
    James! Agatha has told me everything. How cleverly you
    have both kept your secret.

HOPPER

    You don't mind my taking Agatha off to Australia, then,
    Duchess?   355

DUCHESS OF BERWICK (*Indignantly*)

    To Australia? Oh, don't mention that dreadful vulgar
    place.

HOPPER

    But she said she'd like to come with me.

DUCHESS OF BERWICK (*Severely*)

    Did you say that, Agatha?

LADY AGATHA

    Yes, mamma.   360

DUCHESS OF BERWICK

    Agatha, you say the most silly things possible. I think on
    the whole that Grosvenor Square would be a more healthy
    place to reside in. There are lots of vulgar people live in
    Grosvenor Square, but at any rate there are no horrid
    kangaroos crawling about. But we'll talk about that   365
    tomorrow. James, you can take Agatha down. You'll come
    to lunch, of course, James. At half-past one, instead of
    two. The Duke will wish to say a few words to you, I am
    sure.

HOPPER

    I should like to have a chat with the Duke, Duchess. He   370
    has not said a single word to me yet.

DUCHESS OF BERWICK

    I think you'll find he will have a great deal to say to you
    tomorrow. (*Exit* LADY AGATHA *with* MR HOPPER) And now
    goodnight, Margaret. I'm afraid it's the old, old story,

---

350 *Yes, mamma* in T: 'I said "yes", mamma'.

353 *your secret* after this LC has: 'Well, I suppose it must be so. We'll see'.

364 *Grosvenor Square* an ironic reference; the address was eminently respectable in
    the 1890s. Wilde himself had lived there in the 1880s. In 1892 Grosvenor
    Square had 51 addresses. 22 of these had titled tenants.

368–70 *The Duke will wish . . . chat with the Duke, Duchess* i.e., in order to seek
    permission for, and arrange the terms of, the marriage.

dear. Love—well, not love at first sight, but love at the end   375
of the season, which is so much more satisfactory.

LADY WINDERMERE
Goodnight, Duchess.

    Exit the DUCHESS OF BERWICK *on* LORD PAISLEY's *arm*

LADY PLYMDALE
My dear Margaret, what a handsome woman your husband has been dancing with! I should be quite jealous if I
were you! Is she a great friend of yours?   380

LADY WINDERMERE
No!

LADY PLYMDALE
Really? Goodnight, dear.   *Looks at* MR DUMBY *and exit*

DUMBY
Awful manners young Hopper has!

CECIL GRAHAM
Ah! Hopper is one of Nature's gentlemen, the worst type
of gentleman I know.   385

DUMBY
Sensible woman, Lady Windermere. Lots of wives would
have objected to Mrs Erlynne coming. But Lady Windermere has that uncommon thing called common sense.

CECIL GRAHAM
And Windermere knows that nothing looks so like innocence as an indiscretion.   390

DUMBY
Yes; dear Windermere is becoming almost modern. Never
thought he would.   *Bows to* LADY WINDERMERE *and exit*

LADY JEDBURGH
Goodnight, Lady Windermere. What a fascinating woman
Mrs Erlynne is! She is coming to lunch on Thursday,
won't you come too? I expect the Bishop and dear Lady   395
Merton.

LADY WINDERMERE
I am afraid I am engaged, Lady Jedburgh.

375–6 *love at the end of the season* once again making clear the central reason for the
    London Season, for Hopper is the best 'catch' financially. The scenes concern-
    ing the marrying-off of Lady A ironically comment upon the main action by
    seeing sexual relationships primarily in a financial rather than in an emotional
    or ethical context.

387–8 *But Lady Windermere has . . . common sense* LC has 'But Lady Windermere is
    a woman of common sense'.

LADY JEDBURGH
   So sorry. Come, dear.

                    Exeunt LADY JEDBURGH *and* MISS GRAHAM

         Enter MRS ERLYNNE *and* LORD WINDERMERE

MRS ERLYNNE
   Charming ball it has been! Quite reminds me of old days.
   (*Sits on sofa*) And I see that there are just as many fools in   400
   society as there used to be. So pleased to find that nothing
   has altered! Except Margaret. She's grown quite pretty.
   The last time I saw her—twenty years ago, she was a fright
   in flannel. Positive fright, I assure you. The dear Duchess!
   and that sweet Lady Agatha! Just the type of girl I like!   405
   Well, really, Windermere, if I am to be the Duchess's
   sister-in-law—
LORD WINDERMERE (*Sitting L. of her*)
   But are you—?

Exit MR CECIL GRAHAM *with rest of guests.* LADY WINDERMERE
watches, with a look of scorn and pain, MRS ERLYNNE *and her
       husband. They are unconscious of her presence*

MRS ERLYNNE
   Oh, yes! He's to call tomorrow at twelve o'clock! He
   wanted to propose tonight. In fact he did. He kept on   410
   proposing. Poor Augustus, you know how he repeats him-
   self. Such a bad habit! But I told him I wouldn't give him
   an answer till tomorrow. Of course I am going to take him.
   And I daresay I'll make him an admirable wife, as wives
   go. And there is a great deal of good in Lord Augustus.   415
   Fortunately it is all on the surface. Just where good qual-
   ities should be. Of course you must help me in this matter.
LORD WINDERMERE
   I am not called on to encourage Lord Augustus, I suppose?
MRS ERLYNNE
   Oh, no! I do the encouraging. But you will make me a
   handsome settlement, Windermere, won't you?   420
LORD WINDERMERE (*Frowning*)
   Is that what you want to talk to me about tonight?
MRS ERLYNNE
   Yes.

402–4 *Except Margaret . . . I assure you* not in LC. The effect of the omission in LC
   is to remove any suspicion of maternal feeling in Mrs E's comments.
406–7 *Duchess's sister-in-law* and so be in Society.
419–20 *a handsome settlement* i.e., for a dowry.

LORD WINDERMERE (*With a gesture of impatience*)
I will not talk of it here.

MRS ERLYNNE (*Laughing*)
Then we will talk of it on the terrace. Even business should
have a picturesque background. Should it not, Winder- 425
mere? With a proper background women can do anything.

LORD WINDERMERE
Won't tomorrow do as well?

MRS ERLYNNE
No; you see, tomorrow I am going to accept him. And I
think it would be a good thing if I was able to tell him that I
had—well, what shall I say?—£2,000 a year left to me by a 430
third cousin—or a second husband—or some distant relative of that kind. It would be an additional attraction,
wouldn't it? You have a delightful opportunity now of
paying me a compliment, Windermere. But you are not
very clever at paying compliments. I am afraid Margaret 435
doesn't encourage you in that excellent habit. It's a great
mistake on her part. When men give up saying what is
charming, they give up thinking what is charming. But
seriously, what do you say to £2,000? £2,500, I think. In
modern life margin is everything. Windermere, don't you 440
think the world an intensely amusing place? I do!

Exit on terrace with LORD WINDERMERE. *Music strikes up in
ballroom*

LADY WINDERMERE
To stay in this house any longer is impossible. Tonight a
man who loves me offered me his whole life. I refused it. It
was foolish of me. I will offer him mine now. I will give
him mine. I will go to him! (*Puts on cloak and goes to the* 445
*door, then turns back. Sits down at table and writes a letter,
puts it into an envelope, and leaves it on table*) Arthur has
never understood me. When he reads this, he will. He may
do as he chooses now with his life. I have done with mine as

423–6 LORD WINDERMERE
    I will not talk . . . can do anything only in 1st ed.
430–1 *£2,000 a year . . . third cousin* i.e., a sizeable sum, the income from an estate
    of between one and two thousand acres. In all early drafts the cousin is a 'rich
    aunt'.
432–9 *It would be . . . what do you say to* only in 1st ed. and (in a shorter form) C1.
440 *margin is everything* after this LC has 'Let's go on the terrace', so leading the
    audience to believe that her relationship with Lord W *is* illicit.

I think best, as I think right. It is he who has broken the
bond of marriage—not I. I only break its bondage.   450
                                               Exit

PARKER *enters L. and crosses towards the ballroom R. Enter* MRS
ERLYNNE

MRS ERLYNNE
Is Lady Windermere in the ballroom?
PARKER
Her ladyship has just gone out.
MRS ERLYNNE
Gone out? She's not on the terrace?
PARKER
No, madam. Her ladyship has just gone out of the house.
MRS ERLYNNE (*Starts, and looks at the servant with a puzzled
expression in her face*)
Out of the house?   455
PARKER
Yes, madam—her ladyship told me she had left a letter for
his lordship on the table.
MRS ERLYNNE
A letter for Lord Windermere?
PARKER
Yes, madam.
MRS ERLYNNE
Thank you. (*Exit* PARKER. *The music in the ballroom stops*)   460
Gone out of her house! A letter addressed to her husband!
(*Goes over to bureau and looks at letter. Takes it up and lays it
down again with a shudder of fear*) No, no! It would be
impossible! Life doesn't repeat its tragedies like that! Oh,
why does this horrible fancy come across me? Why do I
remember now the one moment of my life I most wish to   465
forget? Does life repeat its tragedies? (*Tears letter open and
reads it, then sinks down into a chair with a gesture of anguish*)
Oh, how terrible! The same words that twenty years ago I
wrote to her father! and how bitterly I have been punished
for it! No; my punishment, my real punishment is tonight,
is now!   *Still seated R.*   470

Enter LORD WINDERMERE *L.U.E.*

458–9 *A letter for . . . Yes, madam* only in 1st ed.
463–6 *Oh, why does . . . to forget* not in LC. The speech in LC is substantially
    different: Lady W's father is called 'my husband', and so the real relationship is
    still hidden. See Introduction and Appendix.

LORD WINDERMERE

Have you said goodnight to my wife?   *Comes C.*

MRS ERLYNNE (*Crushing letter in her hand*)

Yes.

LORD WINDERMERE

Where is she?

MRS ERLYNNE

She is very tired. She has gone to bed. She said she had a
headache.   475

LORD WINDERMERE

I must go to her. You'll excuse me?

MRS ERLYNNE (*Rising hurriedly*)

Oh, no! It's nothing serious. She's only very tired, that is
all. Besides, there are people still in the supper room. She
wants you to make her apologies to them. She said she
didn't wish to be disturbed. (*Drops letter*) She asked me to   480
tell you!

LORD WINDERMERE (*Picks up letter*)

You have dropped something.

MRS ERLYNNE

Oh yes, thank you, that is mine.

                                        Puts out her hand to take it

LORD WINDERMERE (*Still looking at letter*)

But it's my wife's handwriting, isn't it?

MRS ERLYNNE (*Takes the letter quickly*)

Yes, it's—an address. Will you ask them to call my car-   485
riage, please?

LORD WINDERMERE

Certainly.   *Goes L. and exit*

MRS ERLYNNE

Thanks! What can I do? What can I do? I feel a passion
awakening within me that I never felt before. What can it
mean? The daughter must not be like the mother—that   490
would be terrible. How can I save her? How can I save my
child? A moment may ruin a life. Who knows that better
than I? Windermere must be got out of the house; that is
absolutely necessary. (*Goes L.*) But how shall I do it? It
must be done somehow. Ah!   495

   Enter LORD AUGUSTUS *R.U.E. carrying bouquet*

488–93 *I feel a passion . . . better than I* not in LC.

LORD AUGUSTUS

Dear lady, I am in such suspense! May I not have an
answer to my request?

MRS ERLYNNE

Lord Augustus, listen to me. You are to take Lord Windermere down to your club at once, and keep him there as
long as possible. You understand?   500

LORD AUGUSTUS

But you said you wished me to keep early hours!

MRS ERLYNNE (*Nervously*)

Do what I tell you. Do what I tell you.

LORD AUGUSTUS

And my reward?

MRS ERLYNNE

Your reward? Your reward? Oh! ask me that tomorrow.
But don't let Windermere out of your sight tonight. If you 505
do I will never forgive you. I will never speak to you again.
I'll have nothing to do with you. Remember you are to
keep Windermere at your club, and don't let him come
back tonight.   *Exit L.*

LORD AUGUSTUS

Well, really, I might be her husband already. Positively I 510
might.   *Follows her in a bewildered manner*

Act-Drop

496–7 *May I . . . my request* only in 1st ed.

502 *Do what I tell you* LC has instead: 'Oh, don't bother me!'

504–11 *Your reward . . . I might* Mrs E's speech is very different in all the early
drafts of the play. For an account of the revision of these lines see Introduction.
For some of the textual revisions see Appendix.

Act III

Scene: LORD DARLINGTON's *Rooms. A large sofa is in front of fireplace R. At the back of the stage a curtain is drawn across the window. Doors L. and R. Table R. with writing materials. Table C. with syphons, glasses, and Tantalus frame. Table L. with cigar and cigarette-box. Lamps lit*

LADY WINDERMERE (*Standing by the fireplace*)

Why doesn't he come? This waiting is horrible. He should
be here. Why is he not here, to wake by passionate words
some fire within me? I am cold—cold as a loveless thing.
Arthur must have read my letter by this time. If he cared
for me, he would have come after me, would have taken me   5
back by force. But he doesn't care. He's entrammelled by
this woman—fascinated by her—dominated by her. If a
woman wants to hold a man, she has merely to appeal to
what is worst in him. We make gods of men and they leave
us. Others make brutes of them and they fawn and are   10
faithful. How hideous life is! . . . Oh! it was mad of me to
come here, horribly mad. And yet, which is the worst, I
wonder, to be at the mercy of a man who loves one, or the
wife of a man who in one's own house dishonours one?
What woman knows? What woman in the whole world?   15
But will he love me always, this man to whom I am giving
my life? What do I bring him? Lips that have lost the note
of joy, eyes that are blinded by tears, chill hands and icy
heart. I bring him nothing. I must go back—no; I can't go
back, my letter has put me in their power—Arthur would   20
not take me back! That fatal letter! No! Lord Darlington
leaves England tomorrow. I will go with him—I have no
choice. (*Sits down for a few moments. Then starts up and puts*

s.d. These are changed in all drafts of the play. The reference to the Tantalus
frame and its contents is only in 1st ed. It is a 'stand containing usually three
cut-glass decanters which, although apparently free, cannot be withdrawn
until the grooved bar which engages the stoppers is raised' (*OED*).

1–2 *This waiting . . . be here* only in 1st ed. and C1.

9 *We make gods of men* cf. *An Ideal Husband*, II:

SIR ROBERT CHILTERN
. . . Women think that they are making ideals of men. What they are
making of us are false idols merely.

(*An Ideal Husband*, 132 (*CW*, 521))

an inversion of the more usual formula of Society Drama.

11–15 *Oh! it was . . . whole world?* only in 1st ed. and C1.

18–19 *chill hands and an icy heart* not in LC.

on her cloak) No, no! I will go back, let Arthur do with me
what he pleases. I can't wait here. It has been madness my   25
coming. I must go at once. As for Lord Darlington—Oh!
here he is! What shall I do? What can I say to him? Will he
let me go away at all? I have heard that men are brutal,
horrible . . . Oh!   *Hides her face in her hands*

Enter MRS ERLYNNE *L.*

MRS ERLYNNE
Lady Windermere! (LADY WINDERMERE *starts and looks up.*   30
Then recoils in contempt) Thank Heaven I am in time. You
must go back to your husband's house immediately.
LADY WINDERMERE
Must?
MRS ERLYNNE (*Authoritatively*)
Yes, you must! There is not a second to be lost. Lord
Darlington may return at any moment.   35
LADY WINDERMERE
Don't come near me!
MRS ERLYNNE
Oh! You are on the brink of ruin, you are on the brink of a
hideous precipice. You must leave this place at once, my
carriage is waiting at the corner of the street. You must
come with me and drive straight home. (LADY WINDER-   40
MERE *throws off her cloak and flings it on the sofa*) What are
you doing?
LADY WINDERMERE
Mrs Erlynne—if you had not come here, I would have gone
back. But now that I see you, I feel that nothing in the
whole world would induce me to live under the same roof   45
as Lord Windermere. You fill me with horror. There is
something about you that stirs the wildest—rage within
me. And I know why you are here. My husband sent you to
lure me back that I might serve as a blind to whatever
relations exist between you and him.   50

27–9 *What shall I do? . . . Oh!* only in 1st ed. and (in a slightly different form) C1.
37–8 *you are on . . . precipice* only in 1st ed., C1, and BL. Mrs E ironically
    anticipates Lord W in Act IV: 'you may be on the brink of a great sorrow' (viz.
    the possibility of discovering her mother to have been compromised in exactly
    this way).
49–50 *a blind to whatever . . . you and him* a similar sort of domestically convenient
    ménage à trois is proposed in Pinero's *The Notorious Mrs Ebbsmith* (Garrick,
    1895), where for Lucas Cleeve's political success the appearance of domestic
    happiness is essential.

MRS ERLYNNE

Oh! You don't think that—you can't.

LADY WINDERMERE

Go back to my husband, Mrs Erlynne. He belongs to you
and not to me. I suppose he is afraid of a scandal. Men are
such cowards. They outrage every law of the world, and
are afraid of the world's tongue. But he had better prepare   55
himself. He shall have a scandal. He shall have the worst
scandal there has been in London for years. He shall see his
name in every vile paper, mine on every hideous placard.

MRS ERLYNNE

No—no—

LADY WINDERMERE

Yes! he shall. Had he come himself, I admit I would have   60
gone back to the life of degradation you and he had pre-
pared for me—I was going back—but to stay himself at
home, and to send you as his messenger—oh! it was infamous—infamous.

MRS ERLYNNE (*C.*)

Lady Windermere, you wrong me horribly—you wrong   65
your husband horribly. He doesn't know you are here—he
thinks you are safe in your own house. He thinks you are
asleep in your own room. He never read the mad letter you
wrote to him!

LADY WINDERMERE (*R.*)

Never read it!   70

MRS ERLYNNE

No—he knows nothing about it.

LADY WINDERMERE

How simple you think me! (*Going to her*) You are lying to
me!

MRS ERLYNNE (*Restraining herself*)

I am not. I am telling you the truth.

LADY WINDERMERE

If my husband didn't read my letter, how is it that you are   75
here? Who told you I had left the house you were shameless enough to enter? Who told you where I had gone to?
My husband told you, and sent you to decoy me back.

Crosses L.

---

51 *Oh! You don't* before this LC has: 'The relations that exist between him and
me!'

54–5 *They outrage . . . world's tongue* only in 1st ed., Cl, BL, and T.

57–60 *He shall see his name . . . Yes! he shall* only in 1st ed., Cl, and BL.

MRS ERLYNNE (*R.C.*)

Your husband has never seen the letter. I—saw it, I
opened it. I—read it.   80

LADY WINDERMERE (*Turning to her*)

You opened a letter of mine to my husband? You wouldn't
dare!

MRS ERLYNNE

Dare! Oh! to save you from the abyss into which you are
falling, there is nothing in the world I would not dare,
nothing in the whole world. Here is the letter. Your hus-   85
band has never read it. He never shall read it. (*Going to
fireplace*) It should never have been written.

                    Tears it and throws it into the fire

LADY WINDERMERE (*With infinite contempt in her voice and
look*)

How do I know that that was my letter after all? You seem
to think the commonest device can take me in!

MRS ERLYNNE

Oh! why do you disbelieve everything I tell you? What   90
object do you think I have in coming here, except to save
you from utter ruin, to save you from the consequence of a
hideous mistake? That letter that is burnt now *was* your
letter. I swear it to you!

LADY WINDERMERE (*Slowly*)

You took good care to burn it before I had examined it. I   95
cannot trust you. You, whose whole life is a lie, how could
you speak the truth about anything?   *Sits down*

MRS ERLYNNE (*Hurriedly*)

Think as you like about me—say what you choose against
me, but go back, go back to the husband you love.

LADY WINDERMERE (*Sullenly*)

I do *not* love him!   100

MRS ERLYNNE

You do, and you know that he loves you.

LADY WINDERMERE

He does not understand what love is. He understands it as
little as you do—but I see what you want. It would be a
great advantage for you to get me back. Dear Heaven!
what a life I would have then! Living at the mercy of a   105
woman who has neither mercy nor pity in her, a woman

95–6 *I cannot trust you* re-emphasizing the failure of trust which is the root of the
     play's crisis.
96–7 *how could you speak the truth about anything?* only in 1st ed. and C1.

whom it is an infamy to meet, a degradation to know, a vile
woman, a woman who comes between husband and wife!

MRS ERLYNNE (*With a gesture of despair*)

Lady Windermere, Lady Windermere, don't say such terrible things. You don't know how terrible they are, how   110
terrible and how unjust. Listen, you must listen! Only go
back to your husband, and I promise you never to com-
municate with him again on any pretext—never to see
him—never to have anything to do with his life or yours.
The money that he gave me, he gave me not through love,   115
but through hatred, not in worship, but in contempt. The
hold I have over him—

LADY WINDERMERE (*Rising*)

Ah! you admit you have a hold!

MRS ERLYNNE

Yes, and I will tell you what it is. It is his love for you,
Lady Windermere.   120

LADY WINDERMERE

You expect me to believe that?

MRS ERLYNNE

You must believe it! It is true. It is his love for you that has
made him submit to—oh! call it what you like, tyranny,
threats, anything you choose. But it is his love for you. His
desire to spare you—shame, yes, shame and disgrace.   125

LADY WINDERMERE

What do you mean? You are insolent! What have I to do
with you?

MRS ERLYNNE (*Humbly*)

Nothing. I know it—but I tell you that your husband loves
you—that you may never meet with such love again in your
whole life—that such love you will never meet—and that if   130
you throw it away, the day may come when you will starve
for love and it will not be given to you, beg for love and it
will be denied you—Oh! Arthur loves you!

LADY WINDERMERE

Arthur? And you tell me there is nothing between you?

109 *Lady Windermere, Lady Windermere* the repetition is only in 1st ed.

128 *Nothing* Wilde is deliberately reversing a common 19th-century literary
device—the revelation of a blood tie. The plot of *The Importance of Being
Earnest* parodies this convention.

134 *Arthur?* for Mrs E to call Lord W by his Christian name would be proper only if
Mrs E, Lady W, and Lord W were intimately acquainted with each other, and
even then it would be more usual for the absent husband to be referred to by his
surname or title.

MRS ERLYNNE

Lady Windermere, before Heaven your husband is guilt- 135
less of all offence towards you! And I—I tell you that had it
ever occurred to me that such a monstrous suspicion would
have entered your mind, I would have died rather than
have crossed your life or his—oh! died, gladly died!

Moves away to sofa R.

LADY WINDERMERE

You talk as if you had a heart. Women like you have no 140
hearts. Heart is not in you. You are bought and sold.

Sits L.C.

MRS ERLYNNE (*Starts, with a gesture of pain. Then restrains
herself, and comes over to where* LADY WINDERMERE *is sitting.
As she speaks, she stretches out her hands towards her, but does
not dare to touch her*)

Believe what you choose about me. I am not worth a
moment's sorrow. But don't spoil your beautiful young life
on my account! You don't know what may be in store for
you, unless you leave this house at once. You don't know 145
what it is to fall into the pit, to be despised, mocked,
abandoned, sneered at—to be an outcast! to find the door
shut against one, to have to creep in by hideous byways,
afraid every moment lest the mask should be stripped from
one's face, and all the while to hear the laughter, the 150
horrible laughter of the world, a thing more tragic than all
the tears the world has ever shed. You don't know what it
is. One pays for one's sin, and then one pays again, and all
one's life one pays. You must never know that.—As for me,
if suffering be an expiation, then at this moment I have 155
expiated all my faults, whatever they have been; for
tonight you have made a heart in one who had it not, made
it and broken it.—But let that pass. I may have wrecked my
own life, but I will not let you wreck yours. You—why,
you are a mere girl, you would be lost. You haven't got the 160
kind of brains that enables a woman to get back. You have
neither the wit nor the courage. You couldn't stand dis-
honour. No! Go back, Lady Windermere, to the husband
who loves you, whom you love. You have a child, Lady

141 *Heart is not . . . bought and sold* only in 1st ed., Cl, and BL.
147–50 *to find the door . . . and all the while* only in 1st ed. and (in a slightly different
form) C1.
162 *neither the wit nor the courage* it is precisely Mrs E's wit and courage that Lord
and Lady W acknowledge in the final two lines of the play.
164–5 *You have a child, Lady Windermere* only in 1st ed.

Windermere. Go back to that child who even now, in pain   165
or in joy, may be calling to you. (LADY WINDERMERE *rises*)
God gave you that child. He will require from you that you
make his life fine, that you watch over him. What answer
will you make to God if his life is ruined through you? Back
to your house, Lady Windermere—your husband loves   170
you! He has never swerved for a moment from the love he
bears you. But even if he had a thousand loves, you must
stay with your child. If he was harsh to you, you must stay
with your child. If he ill-treated you, you must stay with
your child. If he abandoned you, your place is with your   175
child.

LADY WINDERMERE *bursts into tears and buries her face in her
hands*

(*Rushing to her*) Lady Windermere!
LADY WINDERMERE (*Holding out her hands to her, helplessly, as a
child might do*)
Take me home. Take me home.
MRS ERLYNNE (*Is about to embrace her. Then restrains herself.
There is a look of wonderful joy in her face*)
Come! Where is your cloak? (*Getting it from sofa*) Here. Put
it on. Come at once!   180

They go to the door

LADY WINDERMERE
Stop! Don't you hear voices?
MRS ERLYNNE
No, no! There is no one!
LADY WINDERMERE
Yes, there is! Listen! Oh! that is my husband's voice! He is
coming in! Save me! Oh, it's some plot! You have sent for
him.   *Voices outside*   185
MRS ERLYNNE
Silence! I'm here to save you, if I can. But I fear it is too
late! There! (*Points to the curtain across the window*) The
first chance you have, slip out, if you ever get a chance!
LADY WINDERMERE
But you?

178 *Take me home. Take me home* repetition only in 1st ed., C1, and BL.
183 *Yes, there is! Listen!* after this speech T and LC have:

> LORD WINDERMERE (*Outside*)
> I don't think I can come in.

MRS ERLYNNE

Oh! never mind me. I'll face them.   190

LADY WINDERMERE hides herself behind the curtain

LORD AUGUSTUS (*Outside*)

Nonsense, dear Windermere, you must not leave me!

MRS ERLYNNE

Lord Augustus! Then it is I who am lost!

Hesitates for a moment, then looks round and sees door R., and exit through it

Enter LORD DARLINGTON, MR DUMBY, LORD WINDERMERE, LORD AUGUSTUS LORTON, *and* MR CECIL GRAHAM

DUMBY

What a nuisance their turning us out of the club at this hour! It's only two o'clock. (*Sinks into a chair*) The lively part of the evening is only just beginning.   195

Yawns and closes his eyes

LORD WINDERMERE

It is very good of you, Lord Darlington, allowing Augustus to force our company on you, but I'm afraid I can't stay long.

LORD DARLINGTON

Really! I am so sorry! You'll take a cigar, won't you?

LORD WINDERMERE

Thanks!   *Sits down*   200

LORD AUGUSTUS (*To* LORD WINDERMERE)

My dear boy, you must not dream of going. I have a great deal to talk to you about, of demmed importance, too.

Sits down with him at L. table

CECIL GRAHAM

Oh! We all know what that is! Tuppy can't talk about anything but Mrs Erlynne!

LORD WINDERMERE

Well, that is no business of yours, is it, Cecil?   205

CECIL GRAHAM

None! That is why it interests me. My own business always bores me to death. I prefer other people's.

---

190 *Oh! never mind me* only in 1st ed. and BL. (C1 has 'Never mind about me.')
192 *Then it is I who am lost* because, being in Lord D's room, she would be taken to be his mistress, especially by Lord A.

LORD DARLINGTON

Have something to drink, you fellows. Cecil, you'll have a whisky and soda?

CECIL GRAHAM

Thanks. (*Goes to table with* LORD DARLINGTON) Mrs 210 Erlynne looked very handsome tonight, didn't she?

LORD DARLINGTON

I am not one of her admirers.

CECIL GRAHAM

I usen't to be, but I am now. Why! she actually made me introduce her to poor dear Aunt Caroline. I believe she is going to lunch there.   215

LORD DARLINGTON (*In surprise*)

No?

CECIL GRAHAM

She is, really.

LORD DARLINGTON

Excuse me, you fellows. I'm going away tomorrow. And I have to write a few letters.

Goes to writing table and sits down

DUMBY

Clever woman, Mrs Erlynne.   220

CECIL GRAHAM

Hallo, Dumby! I thought you were asleep.

DUMBY

I am, I usually am!

LORD AUGUSTUS

A very clever woman. Knows perfectly well what a demmed fool I am—knows it as well as I do myself. (CECIL GRAHAM *comes towards him laughing*) Ah! you may laugh, 225 my boy, but it is a great thing to come across a woman who thoroughly understands one.

DUMBY

It is an awfully dangerous thing. They always end by marrying one.

---

209 *whisky and soda* another example of the 'modernity' of Lord D and his friends. The more usually accepted drink had been brandy and soda until the mid-1880s—as, in fact, Lord A drinks below.

212 *I am not one* all drafts have 'I daresay' preceding this line.

214 *Caroline* in all drafts (except C1 where no name is specified) 'Emily'.

226–7 *a woman . . . understands one* picks up Lord D's desire to be misunderstood in Act I and thereby sets Lord A in an ironic contrast with him.

228 *awfully* only in 1st ed.

CECIL GRAHAM

But I thought, Tuppy, you were never going to see her 230
again. Yes! you told me so yesterday evening at the club.
You said you'd heard—   *Whispering to him*

LORD AUGUSTUS

Oh, she's explained that.

CECIL GRAHAM

And the Wiesbaden affair?

LORD AUGUSTUS

She's explained that too.   235

DUMBY

And her income, Tuppy? Has she explained that?

LORD AUGUSTUS (*In a very serious voice*)

She's going to explain that tomorrow.

                              CECIL GRAHAM *goes back to C. table*

DUMBY

Awfully commercial, women nowadays. Our grandmothers threw their caps over the mills, of course, but, by
Jove, their granddaughters only throw their caps over 240
mills that can raise the wind for them.

LORD AUGUSTUS

You want to make her out a wicked woman. She is not!

CECIL GRAHAM

Oh! Wicked women bother one. Good women bore one.
That is the only difference between them.

238–40 *Our grandmothers . . . their granddaughters* only in 1st ed. and C1. The
sentiment looks proverbial, but is not recorded. Colloquially the phrase 'to
throw one's cap over the [wind]mill' is used to indicate over-ambition. After the
speech, C1 has an exchange suggesting the crudest of mercenary motives in
Mrs E's interest in Lord A (so have T and LC):

LORD AUG

Mrs Erlynne knows I haven't got anything.

C. GRAHAM

How does she know?

LORD AUG

Told her so myself.

C. GRAHAM

If you told her so yourself, she won't believe you Tuppy. No one believes
what you say. You have such a poetic, vivid imagination. That is where your
real fascination lies. Mrs Erlynne probably thinks you have millions.

LORD AUGUSTUS (*Puffing a cigar*)

   Mrs Erlynne has a future before her.   245

DUMBY

   Mrs Erlynne has a past before her.

LORD AUGUSTUS

   I prefer women with a past. They're always so demmed amusing to talk to.

CECIL GRAHAM

   Well, you'll have lots of topics of conversation with *her*, Tuppy.   *Rising and going to him*   250

LORD AUGUSTUS

   You're getting annoying, dear boy; you're getting demmed annoying.

CECIL GRAHAM (*Puts his hands on his shoulders*)

   Now, Tuppy, you've lost your figure and you've lost your character. Don't lose your temper; you have only got one.

LORD AUGUSTUS

   My dear boy, if I wasn't the most good-natured man in   255
London—

CECIL GRAHAM

   We'd treat you with more respect, wouldn't we, Tuppy?
                                     Strolls away

DUMBY

   The youth of the present day are quite monstrous. They have absolutely no respect for dyed hair.
                 LORD AUGUSTUS *looks round angrily*

CECIL GRAHAM

   Mrs Erlynne has a very great respect for dear Tuppy.   260

245–6 *Mrs Erlynne has a future . . . past before her* earlier versions of this exchange reveal the way Wilde's witticisms were carefully refined, C1 has:

> LORD AUGUSTUS
>   She's no ordinary woman. She has a future. I believe she has a future.
> LORD DUMBY
>   She's got a past.

And T has:

> LORD A
>   She's no ordinary woman, I can tell you. She's got a future before her—a very remarkable future.
> DUMBY
>   She's got a past, a very remarkable past.

247 *demmed* only in 1st ed. and C1. The following exchange was much revised in the drafts.

DUMBY

Then Mrs Erlynne sets an admirable example to the rest of
her sex. It is perfectly brutal the way most women nowadays behave to men who are not their husbands.

LORD WINDERMERE

Dumby, you are ridiculous, and Cecil, you let your tongue
run away with you. You must leave Mrs Erlynne alone.   265
You don't really know anything about her, and you're
always talking scandal against her.

CECIL GRAHAM (*Coming towards him L.C.*)

My dear Arthur, I never talk scandal. *I* only talk gossip.

LORD WINDERMERE

What is the difference between scandal and gossip?

CECIL GRAHAM

Oh! gossip is charming! History is merely gossip. But   270
scandal is gossip made tedious by morality. Now, I never
moralize. A man who moralizes is usually a hypocrite, and
a woman who moralizes is invariably plain. There is
nothing in the whole world so unbecoming to a woman as a
Nonconformist conscience. And most women know it, I'm   275
glad to say.

LORD AUGUSTUS

Just my sentiments, dear boy, just my sentiments.

CECIL GRAHAM

Sorry to hear it, Tuppy; whenever people agree with me, I
always feel I must be wrong.

LORD AUGUSTUS

My dear boy, when I was your age—   280

CECIL GRAHAM

But you never were, Tuppy, and you never will be. (*Goes
up C.*) I say, Darlington, let us have some cards. You'll
play, Arthur, won't you.

LORD WINDERMERE

No, thanks, Cecil.

261–4 *Then Mrs Erlynne . . . you are ridiculous* only in 1st ed.
268 *talk scandal* LC has after this: 'I wouldn't do such a stupid thing'.
284 *No, thanks, Cecil* here C1 and LC add: 'I never touch cards now'. The line
    appears in T, but is deleted.

DUMBY (*With a sigh*)

Good heavens! how marriage ruins a man! It's as 285
demoralizing as cigarettes, and far more expensive.

CECIL GRAHAM

You'll play, of course, Tuppy?

LORD AUGUSTUS (*Pouring himself out a brandy and soda at table*)

Can't, dear boy. Promised Mrs Erlynne never to play or
drink again.

CECIL GRAHAM

Now, my dear Tuppy, don't be led astray into the paths of 290
virtue. Reformed, you would be perfectly tedious. That is
the worst of women. They always want one to be good.
And if we are good, when they meet us, they don't love us
at all. They like to find us quite irretrievably bad, and to
leave us quite unattractively good. 295

LORD DARLINGTON (*Rising from R. table, where he has been writing letters*)

They always do find us bad!

DUMBY

I don't think we are bad. I think we are all good, except
Tuppy.

LORD DARLINGTON

No, we are all in the gutter, but some of us are looking at
the stars.   *Sits down at C. table* 300

DUMBY

We are all in the gutter, but some of us are looking at the
stars? Upon my word, you are very romantic tonight,
Darlington.

286 *far more expensive* here LC adds:

> LORD WINDERMERE
>
> My dear fellow, cards don't interest me. (*L.*) Besides, it's awfully late. I
> must be getting home. *Rises*
>
> CECIL GRAHAM (*Coming down L.*)
>
> Oh, nonsense, nonsense. The night is only time worth living in. One
> exists during the day, but one lives at night. Well, you'll play of course,
> Tuppy?

C1 is virtually the same.

CECIL GRAHAM
  Too romantic! You must be in love. Who is the girl?
LORD DARLINGTON
  The woman I love is not free, or thinks she isn't.   305
  Glances instinctively at LORD WINDERMERE *while he speaks*
CECIL GRAHAM
  A married woman, then! Well, there's nothing in the world
  like the devotion of a married woman. It's a thing no
  married man knows anything about.
LORD DARLINGTON
  Oh! she doesn't love me. She is a good woman. She is the
  only good woman I have ever met in my life.   310
CECIL GRAHAM
  The only good woman you have ever met in your life?
LORD DARLINGTON
  Yes!
CECIL GRAHAM (*Lighting a cigarette*)
  Well, you are a lucky fellow! Why, I have met hundreds of
  good women. I never seem to meet any but good women.
  The world is perfectly packed with good women. To know   315
  them is a middle-class education.
LORD DARLINGTON
  This woman has purity and innocence. She has everything
  we men have lost.
CECIL GRAHAM
  My dear fellow, what on earth should we men do going

---

304 *Who is the girl?* after this line T (deleted in pencil) has the following exchange
     (BL and C1 are similar):

     LORD AUGUSTUS
       He doesn't love girls.
     DUMBY
         Quite right. I never love girls. They know either too much or too little.

     The deletion points to a feature of other drafts—the representation of London
     Society as obsessed with adultery despite its rigid sexual *mores*.
315–16 *To know them is a middle-class education* the allusion here is to Sir Richard
     Steele's famous 'To love her is a liberal education' in the *Tatler*, 49 (2 August
     1709); Steele's essay is on the difference between love and lust.
317 *This woman has purity* before this BL, C1, and LC have (in slightly differing
     forms): 'This woman makes one better than one is of one's self'.

about with purity and innocence? A carefully thought-out   320
buttonhole is much more effective.

DUMBY

She doesn't really love you then?

LORD DARLINGTON

No, she does not!

DUMBY

I congratulate you, my dear fellow. In this world there are
only two tragedies. One is not getting what one wants, and   325
the other is getting it. The last is much the worst, the last is
a real tragedy! But I am interested to hear she does not love
you. How long could you love a woman who didn't love
you, Cecil?

CECIL GRAHAM

A woman who didn't love me? Oh, all my life!   330

DUMBY

So could I. But it's so difficult to meet one.

LORD DARLINGTON

How can you be so conceited, Dumby?

DUMBY

I didn't say it as a matter of conceit. I said it as a matter of
regret. I have been wildly, madly adored. I am sorry I
have. It has been an immense nuisance. I should like to be   335
allowed a little time to myself now and then.

LORD AUGUSTUS (*Looking round*)

Time to educate yourself, I suppose.

320–1 *A carefully thought-out . . . much more effective* cf. *A Woman of No Importance*,
III:

LORD ILLINGWORTH
The future belongs to the dandy. It is the exquisites who are going to rule.
(*A Woman of No Importance*, 109 (*CW*, 459)).

cf. also *The Importance of Being Earnest*, III, 28–9:

GWENDOLEN
. . . style, not sincerity, is the vital thing.

(*CW*, 371).

After the speech BL, C1, and LC have the following exchange:

LORD DARLINGTON
How corrupt you are, Cecil!
MR GRAHAM
You mean how civilised I am!

327–8 *But I am . . . does not love you* only in 1st ed., and a ms addition to T.

DUMBY

No, time to forget all I have learned. That is much more important, dear Tuppy.

              LORD AUGUSTUS *moves uneasily in his chair*

LORD DARLINGTON

What cynics you fellows are!   340

CECIL GRAHAM

What is a cynic?   *Sitting on the back of the sofa*

LORD DARLINGTON

A man who knows the price of everything and the value of nothing.

CECIL GRAHAM

And a sentimentalist, my dear Darlington, is a man who sees an absurd value in everything, and doesn't know the 345 market price of any single thing.

LORD DARLINGTON

You always amuse me, Cecil. You talk as if you were a man of experience.

CECIL GRAHAM

I am.   *Moves up to front of fireplace*

LORD DARLINGTON

You are far too young!   350

CECIL GRAHAM

That is a great error. Experience is a question of instinct about life. I have got it. Tuppy hasn't. Experience is the name Tuppy gives to his mistakes. That is all.

              LORD AUGUSTUS *looks round indignantly*

DUMBY

Experience is the name everyone gives to their mistakes.

CECIL GRAHAM (*Standing with his back to the fireplace*)

One shouldn't commit any.   355

              Sees LADY WINDERMERE's *fan on sofa*

DUMBY

Life would be very dull without them.

339 *dear Tuppy* only in 1st ed.
341 *What is a cynic?* a much less polished version of this appears in BL:

    LORD DARLINGTON
      Ah! What a young cynic you are!
    MR CECIL GRAHAM
      I know the price of everything.
    LORD DARLINGTON
      And the value of nothing.

CECIL GRAHAM
    Of course you are quite faithful to this woman you are in
    love with, Darlington, to this good woman?
LORD DARLINGTON
    Cecil, if one really loves a woman, all other women in the
    world become absolutely meaningless to one. Love   360
    changes one—*I* am changed.
CECIL GRAHAM
    Dear me! How very interesting! Tuppy, I want to talk to
    you.   LORD AUGUSTUS *takes no notice*
DUMBY
    It's no use talking to Tuppy. You might just as well talk to
    a brick wall.   365
CECIL GRAHAM
    But I like talking to a brick wall—it's the only thing in the
    world that never contradicts me! Tuppy!
LORD AUGUSTUS
    Well, what is it? What is it?
                            Rising and going over to CECIL GRAHAM
CECIL GRAHAM
    Come over here. I want you particularly. (*Aside*) Darling-
    ton has been moralizing and talking about the purity of   370
    love, and that sort of thing, and he has got some woman in
    his rooms all the time.
LORD AUGUSTUS
    No, really! really!
CECIL GRAHAM (*In a low voice*)
    Yes, here is her fan.   *Points to the fan*

359 *Cecil, if one really* before this speech LC has the following exchange:

> LORD DARLINGTON
>   Do you think that a mistake?
> MR GRAHAM
>   Don't love anyone else?   C1 is similar.

368 *What is it?* Before this speech LC has the following exchange:

> LORD AUGUSTUS (*Still seated at table L.C.*)
>   I'm having a serious conversation; I don't want to be disturbed.
> MR GRAHAM
>   Serious conversation is bad for you. It makes you stout.

374 *here is her fan* the presence of a woman's jewellery in a man's room (which
    would be construed as evidence of an adulterous relationship) was a stock
    dramatic mechanism. The use of a fan was not original; contemporary review-
    ers saw Haddon Chambers's *The Idler* as a source in this respect. Alexander had
    produced *The Idler* at the St James's a year earlier (in 1891). But the use of a
    missing object had a long tradition in 19th-century theatre: it was particularly a
    feature of recent French drama (in, for example, Sardou's work).

LORD AUGUSTUS (*Chuckling*)
   By Jove! By Jove!   375
LORD WINDERMERE (*Up by door*)
   I am really off now, Lord Darlington. I am sorry you are
   leaving England so soon. Pray call on us when you come
   back! My wife and I will be charmed to see you!
LORD DARLINGTON (*Up stage with* LORD WINDERMERE)
   I am afraid I shall be away for many years. Goodnight!
CECIL GRAHAM
   Arthur!   380
LORD WINDERMERE
   What?
CECIL GRAHAM
   I want to speak to you for a moment. No, do come!
LORD WINDERMERE (*Putting on his coat*)
   I can't—I'm off!
CECIL GRAHAM
   It is something very particular. It will interest you enorm-
   ously.   385
LORD WINDERMERE (*Smiling*)
   It is some of your nonsense, Cecil.
CECIL GRAHAM
   It isn't! It isn't really.
LORD AUGUSTUS (*Going to him*)
   My dear fellow, you mustn't go yet. I have a lot to talk to
   you about. And Cecil has something to show you.
LORD WINDERMERE (*Walking over*)
   Well, what is it?   390
CECIL GRAHAM
   Darlington has got a woman here in his rooms. Here is her
   fan. Amusing, isn't it?   *A pause*
LORD WINDERMERE
   Good God!   *Seizes the fan*—DUMBY *rises*
CECIL GRAHAM
   What is the matter?
LORD WINDERMERE
   Lord Darlington!   395
LORD DARLINGTON (*Turning round*)
   Yes!
LORD WINDERMERE
   What is my wife's fan doing here in your rooms? Hands off,
   Cecil. Don't touch me.
LORD DARLINGTON
   Your wife's fan?

LORD WINDERMERE
    Yes, here it is!   400

LORD DARLINGTON (*Walking towards him*)
    I don't know!

LORD WINDERMERE
    You must know. I demand an explanation. (*To* CECIL
    GRAHAM) Don't hold me you fool.

LORD DARLINGTON (*Aside*)
    She is here after all!

LORD WINDERMERE
    Speak, sir! Why is my wife's fan here? Answer me! By   405
    God! I'll search your rooms, and if my wife's here, I'll—
                                                          Moves

LORD DARLINGTON
    You shall not search my rooms. You have no right to do so.
    I forbid you!

LORD WINDERMERE
    You scoundrel! I'll not leave your room till I have searched
    every corner of it! What moves behind the curtain?   410
                                  Rushes towards the curtain C.

MRS ERLYNNE (*Enters behind R.*)
    Lord Windermere!

LORD WINDERMERE
    Mrs Erlynne!

Everyone starts and turns round. LADY WINDERMERE *slips out
    from behind the curtain and glides from the room L.*

MRS ERLYNNE
    I am afraid I took your wife's fan in mistake for my own,
    when I was leaving your house tonight. I am so sorry.

Takes fan from him. LORD WINDERMERE *looks at her in contempt.*
LORD DARLINGTON *in mingled astonishment and anger.* LORD
    AUGUSTUS *turns away. The other men smile at each other*

Act-Drop

414 s.d. T and C1 add as a speech at the end of the Act:

    LORD AUGUSTUS
        Oh! this is damned—(*pauses for a word*)—damned!

and so repeat the pattern of a comic ending that Alexander had demanded for
the end of Act II.

Act IV

Scene: Same as in Act I

LADY WINDERMERE (*Lying on sofa*)

How can I tell him? I can't tell him. It would kill me. I
wonder what happened after I escaped from that horrible
room. Perhaps she told them the true reason of her being
there, and the real meaning of that—fatal fan of mine. Oh,
if he knows—how can I look him in the face again? He   5
would never forgive me. (*Touches bell*) How securely one
thinks one lives—out of reach of temptation, sin, folly.
And then suddenly—Oh! Life is terrible. It rules us, we do
not rule it.   *Complex view of world.*

Enter ROSALIE *R.*

ROSALIE

Did your ladyship ring for me?   10

LADY WINDERMERE

Yes. Have you found out at what time Lord Windermere
came in last night?

ROSALIE

His lordship did not come in till five o'clock.

LADY WINDERMERE

Five o'clock? He knocked at my door this morning, didn't
he?   15

ROSALIE

Yes, my lady—at half-past nine. I told him your ladyship
was not awake yet.

LADY WINDERMERE

Did he say anything?

ROSALIE

Something about your ladyship's fan. I didn't quite catch
what his lordship said. Has the fan been lost, my lady? I   20
can't find it, and Parker says it was not left in any of the
rooms. He has looked in all of them and on the terrace as
well.

1 s.d. *Scene* C1, T, and LC set the act in Lady W's boudoir.
8–9 *Life is terrible . . . not rule it* Lady W's sentiment contrasts strongly with
those of the dandy, whose control over life has an analogue in the artist's control
over his material.

LADY WINDERMERE
  It doesn't matter. Tell Parker not to trouble. That will do.

                                                          Exit ROSALIE

LADY WINDERMERE (*Rising*)
  She is sure to tell him. I can fancy a person doing a   25
  wonderful act of self-sacrifice, doing it spontaneously,
  recklessly, nobly—and afterwards finding out that it costs
  too much. Why should she hesitate between her ruin and
  mine? . . . How strange! I would have publicly disgraced
  her in my own house. She accepts public disgrace in the   30
  house of another to save me. . . . There is a bitter irony in
  things, a bitter irony in the way we talk of good and bad
  women. . . . Oh, what a lesson! and what a pity that in life
  we only get our lessons when they are of no use to us! For
  even if she doesn't tell, I must. Oh! the shame of it, the   35
  shame of it. To tell it is to live through it all again. Actions
  are the first tragedy in life, words are the second. Words
  are perhaps the worst. Words are merciless. . . . Oh!

                              Starts as LORD WINDERMERE *enters*

LORD WINDERMERE (*Kisses her*)
  Margaret—how pale you look!

LADY WINDERMERE
  I slept very badly.   40

LORD WINDERMERE (*Sitting on sofa with her*)
  I am so sorry. I came in dreadfully late, and didn't like to
  wake you. You are crying, dear.

LADY WINDERMERE
  Yes, I am crying, for I have something to tell you, Arthur.

LORD WINDERMERE
  My dear child, you are not well. You've been doing too
  much. Let us go away to the country. You'll be all right at   45
  Selby. The season is almost over. There is no use staying

---

25 *She is sure to tell him* before this LC has: 'Perhaps he's gone to Curzon Street!'
   C1 is similar.
29–34 *How strange . . . no use to us* only in 1st ed. and (in a slightly different form)
   C1.
45–6 *Let us go away . . . almost over* another socially precise comment, for usually
   members of Society spent the Season in London and then returned to their
   country homes for various country sports (like shooting) and to attend to
   country affairs. For the way in which Selby is used in the play see note to I, 12.

on. Poor darling! We'll go away today, if you like. (*Rises*)
We can easily catch the 3.40. I'll send a wire to Fannen.

    Crosses and sits down at table to write a telegram

LADY WINDERMERE

Yes; let us go away today. No; I can't go today, Arthur.
There is someone I must see before I leave town—someone   50
who has been kind to me.

LORD WINDERMERE (*Rising and leaning over sofa*)

Kind to you?

LADY WINDERMERE

Far more than that. (*Rises and goes to him*) I will tell you,
Arthur, but only love me, love me as you used to love me.

LORD WINDERMERE

Used to? You are not thinking of that wretched woman   55
who came here last night? (*Coming round and sitting R. of
her*) You don't still imagine—no, you couldn't.

LADY WINDERMERE

I don't. I know now I was wrong and foolish.

LORD WINDERMERE

It was very good of you to receive her last night—but you
are never to see her again.   60

LADY WINDERMERE

Why do you say that?   *A pause*

LORD WINDERMERE (*Holding her hand*)

Margaret, I thought Mrs Erlynne was a woman more
sinned against than sinning, as the phrase goes. I thought
she wanted to be good, to get back into a place that she had
lost by a moment's folly, to lead again a decent life. I   65
believed what she told me—I was mistaken in her. She is
bad—as bad as a woman can be.

LADY WINDERMERE

Arthur, Arthur, don't talk so bitterly about any woman. I
don't think now that people can be divided into the good
and the bad, as though they were two separate races or   70

46–7 *staying on* following this sentence, LC has:

    We'll go next week.
    LADY WINDERMERE
      Oh, before that! I am bewildered with life—it frightens me!

C1 is substantially the same.

68–74 *I don't think . . . repentance, pity, sacrifice* of the drafts, only in BL, C1, LC,
and T (where it occurs in a slightly different form). This constitutes the most
overt statement of the play's central theme of the possible discrepancy between
social and moral values.

creations. What are called good women may have terrible
things in them, mad moods of recklessness, assertion,
jealousy, sin. Bad women, as they are termed, may have in
them sorrow, repentance, pity, sacrifice. And I don't think
Mrs Erlynne a bad woman—I know she's not. 75

LORD WINDERMERE

My dear child, the woman's impossible. No matter what
harm she tries to do us, you must never see her again. She
is inadmissible anywhere.

LADY WINDERMERE

But I want to see her. I want her to come here.

LORD WINDERMERE

Never! 80

LADY WINDERMERE

She came here once as *your* guest. She must come now as
mine. That is but fair.

LORD WINDERMERE

She should never have come here.

LADY WINDERMERE (*Rising*)

It is too late, Arthur, to say that now. *Moves away*

LORD WINDERMERE (*Rising*)

Margaret, if you knew where Mrs Erlynne went last night, 85
after she left this house, you would not sit in the same room
with her. It was absolutely shameless, the whole thing.

LADY WINDERMERE

Arthur, I can't bear it any longer. I must tell you. Last
night—

Enter PARKER *with a tray on which lie* LADY WINDERMERE's
fan and a card

PARKER

Mrs Erlynne has called to return your ladyship's fan which 90
she took away by mistake last night. Mrs Erlynne has
written a message on the card.

LADY WINDERMERE

Oh, ask Mrs Erlynne to be kind enough to come up. (*Reads
card*) Say I shall be very glad to see her. *Exit* PARKER
She wants to see me, Arthur. 95

77–8 *She is inadmissible anywhere* of the drafts, only in T and C1 (but the early part
of the speech is substantially altered in both drafts). The 1st ed. draws upon
elements in all mss.

LORD WINDERMERE (*Takes card and looks at it*)

Margaret, I *beg* you not to. Let me see her first, at any rate.
She's a very dangerous woman. She is the most dangerous
woman I know. You don't realize what you're doing.

LADY WINDERMERE

It is right that I should see her.

LORD WINDERMERE

My child, you may be on the brink of a great sorrow. Don't 100
go to meet it. It is absolutely necessary that I should see her
before you do.

LADY WINDERMERE

Why should it be necessary?

Enter PARKER

PARKER

Mrs Erlynne.

Enter MRS ERLYNNE

Exit PARKER

MRS ERLYNNE

How do you do, Lady Windermere? (*To* LORD WINDER- 105
MERE) How do you do? Do you know, Lady Windermere,
I am so sorry about your fan. I can't imagine how I made
such a silly mistake. Most stupid of me. And as I was
driving in your direction, I thought I would take the
opportunity of returning your property in person with 110
many apologies for my carelessness, and of bidding you
goodbye.

LADY WINDERMERE

Goodbye? (*Moves towards sofa with* MRS ERLYNNE *and sits
down beside her*) Are you going away, then, Mrs Erlynne?

MRS ERLYNNE

Yes; I am going to live abroad again. The English climate 115
doesn't suit me. My—heart is affected here, and that I

97–8 *She is the most dangerous woman I know* only in 1st ed. and C1.

103 *Why should it be necessary?* LC has simply 'Why?'

108–9 *I was driving in your direction* only in 1st ed.

110 *in person* only in 1st ed.

114 *then* only in 1st ed. The additions to the 1st ed. once more reveal Wilde's care in
revision.

115 *to live abroad again* the reference to foreign travel as a socially convenient device
is made explicit in Mrs E's ironic reference to her 'heart'.

don't like. I prefer living in the south. London is too full of
fogs and—and serious people, Lord Windermere.
Whether the fogs produce the serious people or whether
the serious people produce the fogs, I don't know, but the   120
whole thing rather gets on my nerves, and so I'm leaving
this afternoon by the Club Train.

LADY WINDERMERE

This afternoon? But I wanted so much to come and see
you.

MRS ERLYNNE

How kind of you! But I am afraid I have to go.   125

LADY WINDERMERE

Shall I never see you again, Mrs Erlynne?

MRS ERLYNNE

I am afraid not. Our lives lie too far apart. But there is a
little thing I would like you to do for me. I want a photograph of you, Lady Windermere—would you give me one?
You don't know how gratified I should be.   130

LADY WINDERMERE

Oh, with pleasure. There is one on that table. I'll show it to
you.   *Goes across to the table*

LORD WINDERMERE (*Coming up to* MRS ERLYNNE *and speaking
in a low voice*)

It is monstrous your intruding yourself here after your
conduct last night.

MRS ERLYNNE (*With an amused smile*)

My dear Windermere, manners before morals!   135

117–20 *London is too full of fogs . . . produce the fogs* a familiar joke. cf. 'The Decay of
Lying':

> VIVIAN
> . . . Where, if not from the Impressionists, do we get those wonderful
> brown fogs that come creeping down our streets.
>
> (*Intentions*, 41 (*CW*, 986))

118 *serious people* cf. Lord D's affectation of flippancy to safeguard a private
seriousness: 'Life is far too important a thing ever to talk seriously about it' (I,
190–1). Mrs E's frivolity is also more literally a fidelity to serious feeling by
protecting her daughter.

122 *by the Club Train* T, BL, C1, LC make the last sentence another speech for Mrs
E. 'Club trains' were luxurious expresses from London's Cannon Street to
Dover, inaugurated to connect London with Paris for the 1889 Paris Exhi-
bition. They left London at 4.00 p.m. and arrived in Paris at 11.30 p.m. They
ran between 1889 and 1893.

135 *My dear Windermere, manners before morals* another reference to the central
theme. Mrs E is right, for the host (Lord W) is insulting her (the guest). T and
LC have simply 'Really!'

LADY WINDERMERE (*Returning*)

I'm afraid it is very flattering—I am not so pretty as that.

Showing photograph

MRS ERLYNNE

You are much prettier. But haven't you got one of yourself with your little boy?

LADY WINDERMERE

I have. Would you prefer one of those?

MRS ERLYNNE

Yes.   140

LADY WINDERMERE

I'll go and get it for you, if you'll excuse me for a moment. I have one upstairs.

MRS ERLYNNE

So sorry, Lady Windermere, to give you so much trouble.

LADY WINDERMERE (*Moves to door R.*)

No trouble at all, Mrs Erlynne.

MRS ERLYNNE

Thanks so much.   *Exit* LADY WINDERMERE *R.*   145

You seem rather out of temper this morning, Windermere. Why should you be? Margaret and I get on charmingly together.

LORD WINDERMERE

I can't bear to see you with her. Besides, you have not told me the truth, Mrs Erlynne.   150

MRS ERLYNNE

I have not told *her* the truth, you mean.

LORD WINDERMERE (*Standing C.*)

I sometimes wish you had. I should have been spared then the misery, the anxiety, the annoyance of the last six months. But rather than my wife should know—that the mother whom she was taught to consider as dead, the   155 mother whom she has mourned as dead, is living—a divorced woman, going about under an assumed name, a bad woman preying upon life, as I know you now to be—rather than that, I was ready to supply you with money to pay bill after bill, extravagance after extrava-   160 gance, to risk what occurred yesterday, the first quarrel I have ever had with my wife. You don't understand what that means to me. How could you? But I tell you that the

---

147 *Margaret and I* only in 1st ed.; in most early drafts 'your wife'.

152 *I sometimes wish you had* in the LC text this speech is the first revelation of the real identity of Mrs E.

158 *preying upon life* only in 1st ed., BL, and C1.

only bitter words that ever came from those sweet lips of
hers were on your account, and I hate to see you next her. 165
You sully the innocence that is in her. (*Moves L.C.*) And
then I used to think that with all your faults you were frank
and honest. You are not.

MRS ERLYNNE
Why do you say that?

LORD WINDERMERE
You made me get you an invitation to my wife's ball.   170

MRS ERLYNNE
For my daughter's ball—yes.

LORD WINDERMERE
You came, and within an hour of your leaving the house
you are found in a man's rooms—you are disgraced before
everyone.   *Goes up stage C.*

MRS ERLYNNE
Yes.   175

LORD WINDERMERE (*Turning round on her*)
Therefore I have a right to look upon you as what you
are—a worthless, vicious woman. I have the right to tell
you never to enter this house, never to attempt to come
near my wife—

MRS ERLYNNE (*Coldly*)
My daughter, you mean.   180

LORD WINDERMERE
You have no right to claim her as your daughter. You left
her, abandoned her when she was but a child in the cradle,
abandoned her for your lover, who abandoned you in turn.

MRS ERLYNNE (*Rising*)
Do you count that to his credit, Lord Windermere—or to
mine?   185

LORD WINDERMERE
To his, now that I know you.

MRS ERLYNNE
Take care—you had better be careful.

LORD WINDERMERE
Oh, I am not going to mince words for you. I know you
thoroughly.

MRS ERLYNNE (*Looking steadily at him*)
I question that.   190

166–7 *And then* only in 1st ed., BL, and C1.
167 *with all your faults* only in 1st ed.
175 *Yes* LC has: 'that is no doubt true'. C1 is similar.

[handwritten: judge her morals]

LORD WINDERMERE

I *do* know you. For twenty years of your life you lived without your child, without a thought of your child. One day you read in the papers that she had married a rich man. You saw your hideous chance. You knew that to spare her the ignominy of learning that a woman like you was her				195
mother, I would endure anything. You began your black-mailing.

MRS ERLYNNE (*Shrugging her shoulders*)

Don't use ugly words, Windermere. They are vulgar. I saw my chance, it is true, and took it. *[handwritten: ← opportunity]*

LORD WINDERMERE

Yes, you took it—and spoiled it all last night by being				200
found out.

MRS ERLYNNE (*With a strange smile*)

You are quite right, I spoiled it all last night.

LORD WINDERMERE

And as for your blunder in taking my wife's fan from here and then leaving it about in Darlington's rooms, it is unpardonable. I can't bear the sight of it now. I shall never				205
let my wife use it again. The thing is soiled for me. You should have kept it and not brought it back.

MRS ERLYNNE

I think I *shall* keep it. (*Goes up*) It's extremely pretty. (*Takes up fan*) I shall ask Margaret to give it to me.

LORD WINDERMERE

I hope my wife will give it you.				210

MRS ERLYNNE

Oh, I'm sure she will have no objection.

LORD WINDERMERE

I wish that at the same time she would give you a miniature she kisses every night before she prays—It's the miniature of a young innocent-looking girl with beautiful dark hair.

MRS ERLYNNE

Ah, yes, I remember. How long ago that seems! (*Goes to*				215
sofa and sits down) It was done before I was married. Dark hair and an innocent expression were the fashion then, Windermere!				*A pause*

[handwritten: appearance is everything – an act]

194 *hideous* only in 1st ed. and C1.

202 *You are quite right* only in 1st ed.; T, F, Cms, C2, and LC simply have: 'Yes.'

210 *I hope my wife will give it you* T and C1 have: 'I hope to goodness she will'.

214 *beautiful dark hair* T: 'dark hair'; C2: 'wonderful black hair'; F and LC have: 'wonderful dark hair'.

217 *fashion then, Windermere* 'Windermere' only in 1st ed.

LORD WINDERMERE

What do you mean by coming here this morning? What is
your object?   *Crossing L.C. and sitting*   220

MRS ERLYNNE (*With a note of irony in her voice*)

To bid goodbye to my dear daughter, of course. (LORD
WINDERMERE *bites his under-lip in anger.* MRS ERLYNNE *looks
at him, and her voice and manner become serious. In her accents
as she talks there is a note of deep tragedy. For a moment she
reveals herself*) Oh, don't imagine I am going to have a
pathetic scene with her, weep on her neck and tell her who
I am, and all that kind of thing. I have no ambition to play
the part of a mother. Only once in my life have I known a   225
mother's feelings. That was last night. They were terrible—they made me suffer—they made me suffer too
much. For twenty years, as you say, I have lived childless,—I want to live childless still. (*Hiding her feelings with
a trivial laugh*) Besides, my dear Windermere, how on   230
earth could I pose as a mother with a grown-up daughter?
Margaret is twenty-one, and I have never admitted that I
am more than twenty-nine, or thirty at the most.
Twenty-nine when there are pink shades, thirty when
there are not. So you see what difficulties it would involve.   235
No, as far as I am concerned, let your wife cherish the
memory of this dead, stainless mother. Why should I
interfere with her illusions? I find it hard enough to keep
my own. I lost one illusion last night. I thought I had no
heart. I find I have, and a heart doesn't suit me, Winder-   240
mere. Somehow it doesn't go with modern dress. It makes
one look old. (*Takes up hand-mirror from table and looks into
it*) And it spoils one's career at critical moments.

LORD WINDERMERE

You fill me with horror—with absolute horror.

MRS ERLYNNE (*Rising*)

I suppose, Windermere, you would like me to retire into a   245
convent or become a hospital nurse, or something of that

221 *To bid* T and C1 (deleted in pencil) have: 'I came simply to bid'.

222–43 *Oh, don't imagine . . . critical moments* the situation that Wilde is exploiting
is one very familiar in 19th-century fiction and drama—the final and climactic
revelation of a blood-tie that explains hitherto bizarre actions. But by avoiding
a declaration of the real relationship, Wilde is resisting the sentimentality of the
convention.

242 *look old* following this sentence T and C1 have 'Yes; it positively gives one
wrinkles under one's eyes. Those who live for pleasure, Windermere, as I
do—as all sensible people do—should have no hearts'. Its deletion makes Mrs
E a much less mercenary figure.

plays

kind, as people do in silly modern novels. That is stupid of
you, Arthur; in real life we don't do such things—not as
long as we have any good looks left, at any rate. No—what
consoles one nowadays is not repentance, but pleasure.　250
Repentance is quite out of date. And besides, if a woman
really repents, she has to go to a bad dressmaker, otherwise
no one believes in her. And nothing in the world would
induce me to do that. No; I am going to pass entirely out of
your two lives. My coming into them has been a mistake—I　255
discovered that last night.

LORD WINDERMERE
　A fatal mistake.

MRS ERLYNNE (*Smiling*)
　Almost fatal.

undermine
conventions.

247 *silly modern novels* T and C1 have 'silly English novels and silly French plays'.
　　Perhaps the reference to French plays would have reminded a contemporary
　　audience of the origins of some of the features of Wilde's play.

248–9 *in real life* . . . *at any rate* T and C1 have in addition: 'We go to Homburg, or
　　Paris, or Aix, or some place where we can amuse ourselves'.

254 *induce me to do that* not in LC. After the line T has: 'Believe me, my dear
　　Windermere, you take life too seriously and so does your wife. Nothing matters
　　much in the nineteenth century, except want of money.

　　　　LORD WINDERMERE
　　　　　I suppose you have come for that.
　　　　MRS ERLYNNE
　　　　　No: oddly enough, I haven't. I am never going to ask you for any money
　　　　　again.'

　　BL, Cms, C1, and C2 are substantially the same.

257–8 *A fatal mistake* . . . *Almost fatal* only in 1st ed. The next lines are substan-
　　tially different in T. Instead of this exchange LC has:

　　　　LORD WINDERMERE
　　　　　I'm glad you have that amount of feeling in you.
　　　　MRS ERLYNNE
　　　　　I have that amount! And so, Arthur, when my daughter comes back I will
　　　　　bid you both goodbye, and I don't think we shall ever meet again.
　　　　LORD WINDERMERE
　　　　　I am very glad to hear it. But you don't realize what you have made me go
　　　　　through.
　　　　MRS ERLYNNE
　　　　　The worries of other people can hardly be supposed to interest a woman
　　　　　like me.

　　C1 is substantially the same.

LORD WINDERMERE

I am sorry now I did not tell my wife the whole thing at
once.　　　　　　　　　　　　　　　　　　　　　　260

MRS ERLYNNE

I regret my bad actions. You regret your good ones—that is
the difference between us.

LORD WINDERMERE

I don't trust you. I *will* tell my wife. It's better for her to
know, and from me. It will cause her infinite pain—it will
humiliate her terribly, but it's right that she should know.　265

MRS ERLYNNE

You propose to tell her?

LORD WINDERMERE

I am going to tell her.

MRS ERLYNNE (*Going up to him*)

If you do, I will make my name so infamous that it will mar
every moment of her life. It will ruin her, and make her
wretched. If you dare to tell her, there is no depth of　270
degradation I will not sink to, no pit of shame I will not
enter. You shall not tell her—I forbid you.

LORD WINDERMERE

Why?

MRS ERLYNNE (*After a pause*)　*martyr because of Motherhood .*

If I said to you that I cared for her, perhaps loved her
even—you would sneer at me, wouldn't you?　　　　275

LORD WINDERMERE

I should feel it was not true. A mother's love means devotion, unselfishness, sacrifice. What could you know of
such things?

MRS ERLYNNE

You are right. What could I know of such things? Don't let

268　*my name so infamous* once more, Mrs E is playing private morality against public
　　reputation. For a similar ploy see C. H. Hazlewood's adaptation of Mary
　　Braddon's *Lady Audley's Secret* (Royal Victoria, 1863) II, i:

　　　　LADY AUDLEY
　　　　. . . Even if your suspicions are right, what good will it do you? I will tell
　　　　you; it will break your uncle's heart, and disgrace his family, tarnish the
　　　　escutcheon of the proud Audley family, and leave a stain on the race
　　　　forever.

268–9　*mar every moment . . . her life* for this LC has: 'it will be a daily horror to her'.
270–2　*If you dare to tell her . . . enter* only in 1st ed. and C1.
276　*not true* after this sentence C1, T, and LC have: 'What could you understand of
　　the sort of love a mother should have for her child? Nothing! Love like that
　　means things that are hidden from you, that will be always hidden from you'.

us talk any more about it—as for telling my daughter who I   280
am, that I do not allow. It is my secret, it is not yours. If I
make up my mind to tell her, and I think I will, I shall tell
her before I leave the house—if not, I shall never tell her.

LORD WINDERMERE (*Angrily*)

Then let me beg of you to leave our house at once. I will
make your excuses to Margaret.   285

Enter LADY WINDERMERE *R. She goes over to* MRS ERLYNNE
with the photograph in her hand. LORD WINDERMERE *moves to
back of sofa, and anxiously watches* MRS ERLYNNE *as the scene
progresses*

LADY WINDERMERE

I am so sorry, Mrs Erlynne, to have kept you waiting. I
couldn't find the photograph anywhere. At last I discovered it in my husband's dressing-room—he had stolen
it.

MRS ERLYNNE (*Takes the photograph from her and looks at it*)

I am not surprised—it is charming. (*Goes over to sofa with*   290
LADY WINDERMERE, *and sits down beside her. Looks again at
the photograph*) And so that is your little boy! What is he
called?

LADY WINDERMERE

Gerard, after my dear father.

MRS ERLYNNE (*Laying the photograph down*)

Really?

LADY WINDERMERE

Yes. If it had been a girl, I would have called it after my   295
mother. My mother had the same name as myself, Margaret.

MRS ERLYNNE

My name is Margaret too.

LADY WINDERMERE

Indeed!

MRS ERLYNNE

Yes. (*Pause*) You are devoted to your mother's memory,   300
Lady Windermere, your husband tells me.

LADY WINDERMERE

We all have ideals in life. At least we all should have. Mine
is my mother.

MRS ERLYNNE

Ideals are dangerous things. Realities are better. They
wound, but they're better.   305

281 *not yours* after this LC has 'and if I choose to forget it, you have nothing to say in
the matter'.

LADY WINDERMERE (*Shaking her head*)
  If I lost my ideals, I should lose everything.

MRS ERLYNNE
  Everything?

LADY WINDERMERE
  Yes.   *Pause*

MRS ERLYNNE
  Did your father often speak to you of your mother?

LADY WINDERMERE
  No, it gave him too much pain. He told me how my mother   310
had died a few months after I was born. His eyes filled with
tears as he spoke. Then he begged me never to mention her
name to him again. It made him suffer even to hear it. My
father—my father really died of a broken heart. His was the
most ruined life I know.   315

MRS ERLYNNE (*Rising*)
  I am afraid I must go now, Lady Windermere.

LADY WINDERMERE (*Rising*)
  Oh no, don't.

MRS ERLYNNE
  I think I had better. My carriage must have come back by
this time. I sent it to Lady Jedburgh's with a note.

LADY WINDERMERE
  Arthur, would you mind seeing if Mrs Erlynne's carriage   320
has come back?

MRS ERLYNNE
  Pray don't trouble, Lord Windermere.

LADY WINDERMERE
  Yes, Arthur, do go, please.

310 *too much pain* C1 and T add here: 'I remember once when I was about six years
    of age asking him why all the other children I used to play with had mothers
    while I had none.

      MRS ERLYNNE
        And what did he say?
      LADY WINDERMERE
        He told me . . .'

    LC is similar.

314–15 *His was the most ruined life I know* of early drafts only in C1, T, and LC. The
    following lines are very different in C1.

322–4 *Pray don't trouble . . . Oh!* not in F or LC; ms addition to T. In II Lord W
    willingly (and, according to etiquette, correctly) calls Mrs E's carriage at her
    request. Here, of course, not only does he believe that she has relinquished her
    right to be so treated, but he doesn't want to leave Mrs E alone with Lady W
    since he still takes her to be a corrupting influence.

LORD WINDERMERE *hesitates for a moment and looks at* MRS
ERLYNNE. *She remains quite impassive. He leaves the room*

(*To* MRS ERLYNNE) Oh! What am I to say to you? You saved
   me last night.   *Goes towards her* 325
MRS ERLYNNE
   Hush—don't speak of it.
LADY WINDERMERE
   I must speak of it. I can't let you think that I am going to
   accept this sacrifice. I am not. It is too great. I am going to
   tell my husband everything. It is my duty.
MRS ERLYNNE
   It is not your duty—at least you have duties to others 330
   besides him. You say you owe me something?
LADY WINDERMERE
   I owe you everything.
MRS ERLYNNE
   Then pay your debt by silence. That is the only way in
   which it can be paid. Don't spoil the one good thing I have
   done in my life by telling it to anyone. Promise me that 335
   what passed last night will remain a secret between us. You
   must not bring misery into your husband's life. Why spoil
   his love? You must not spoil it. Love is easily killed. Oh!
   how easily love is killed! Pledge me your word, Lady
   Windermere, that you will *never* tell him. I insist upon it. 340
LADY WINDERMERE (*With bowed head*)
   It is your will, not mine.
MRS ERLYNNE
   Yes, it is my will. And never forget your child—I like to
   think of you as a mother. I like you to think of yourself as
   one.
LADY WINDERMERE (*Looking up*)
   I always will now. Only once in my life I have forgotten my 345

324–5 *You saved me last night.* after this T has: 'you sacrificed yourself for me. You
    bore the burden of my sin'.
333–4 *That is the only . . . be paid* not in LC.
335 *telling it to anyone* in C1 the speech ends here. T is more elaborate and has:
    'Besides a scandal is my proper ending, I fear, Lady Windermere' (C1 also has
    this line).
338–9 *Oh! how easily love is killed* only in 1st ed.
341 *It is your . . . mine* before this sentence, LC has: 'I pledge you my word'.
342–4 *And never . . . as one* instead of this speech LC has: 'And never forget you are
    a mother. There was a woman I knew once—but never mind about her. You
    must always remember that you are a mother'.

own mother—that was last night. Oh, if I had remembered
her I should not have been so foolish, so wicked.

MRS ERLYNNE (*With a slight shudder*)

Hush, last night is quite over.

Enter LORD WINDERMERE

LORD WINDERMERE

Your carriage has not come back yet, Mrs Erlynne.

MRS ERLYNNE

It makes no matter. I'll take a hansom. There is nothing in   350
the world so respectable as a good Shrewsbury and Talbot.
And now, dear Lady Windermere, I am afraid it is really
goodbye. (*Moves up C.*) Oh, I remember. You'll think me
absurd, but do you know I've taken a great fancy to this fan
that I was silly enough to run away with last night from   355
your ball. Now, I wonder would you give it to me? Lord
Windermere says you may. I know it is his present.

LADY WINDERMERE

Oh, certainly, if it will give you any pleasure. But it has my
name on it. It has 'Margaret' on it.

MRS ERLYNNE

But we have the same Christian name.   360

LADY WINDERMERE

Oh, I forgot. Of course, do have it. What a wonderful
chance our names being the same!

MRS ERLYNNE

Quite wonderful. Thanks—it will always remind me of
you.   *Shakes hands with her*

Enter PARKER

PARKER

Lord Augustus Lorton. Mrs Erlynne's carriage has come.   365

Enter LORD AUGUSTUS

LORD AUGUSTUS

Good morning, dear boy. Good morning, Lady Windermere. (*Sees* MRS ERLYNNE) Mrs Erlynne!

350–1 *There is nothing . . . a Shrewsbury and Talbot* only in 1st ed. Lord
     Shrewsbury and Talbot's rubber-tyred and luxuriously appointed cabs were
     introduced about 1880. They were the quietest and most comfortable cabs of
     the time. As the wheels were noiseless, the cabs were immensely popular.
365 *Mrs Erlynne's carriage has come* only in 1st ed.
367 *Mrs Erlynne!* C1, T, and LC have instead: 'Good—good Heavens!'

MRS ERLYNNE
> How do you do, Lord Augustus? Are you quite well this morning?

LORD AUGUSTUS (*Coldly*)
> Quite well, thank you, Mrs Erlynne.   370

MRS ERLYNNE
> You don't look at all well, Lord Augustus. You stop up too late—it is so bad for you. You really should take more care of yourself. Goodbye, Lord Windermere. (*Goes towards door with a bow to* LORD AUGUSTUS. *Suddenly smiles and looks back at him*) Lord Augustus! Won't you see me to my carriage? You might carry the fan.   375

LORD WINDERMERE
> Allow me!

MRS ERLYNNE
> No; I want Lord Augustus. I have a special message for the dear Duchess. Won't you carry the fan, Lord Augustus?

LORD AUGUSTUS
> If you really desire it, Mrs Erlynne.   380

MRS ERLYNNE (*Laughing*)
> Of course I do. You'll carry it so gracefully. You would carry off anything gracefully, dear Lord Augustus.

When she reaches the door she looks back for a moment at LADY
WINDERMERE. *Their eyes meet. Then she turns, and exit C.*
followed by LORD AUGUSTUS

LADY WINDERMERE
> You will never speak against Mrs Erlynne again, Arthur, will you?

LORD WINDERMERE (*Gravely*)
> She is better than one thought her.   385

LADY WINDERMERE
> She is better than I am.

LORD WINDERMERE (*Smiling as he strokes her hair*)
> Child, you and she belong to different worlds. Into your world evil has never entered.

LADY WINDERMERE
> Don't say that, Arthur. There is the same world for all of us, and good and evil, sin and innocence, go through it   390

---

375 *might carry the fan* C1 and LC have: 'Won't you see me to my brougham? You might carry the fan. I think you'd look delightful carrying the fan'.
381–2 *You would carry . . . dear Lord Augustus* not in LC.

hand in hand. To shut one's eyes to half of life that one may
live securely is as though one blinded oneself that one
might walk with more safety in a land of pit and precipice.

LORD WINDERMERE (*Moves down with her*)

Darling, why do you say that?

LADY WINDERMERE (*Sits on sofa*)

Because I, who had shut my eyes to life, came to the brink.   395
And one who had separated us—

LORD WINDERMERE

We were never separated.

LADY WINDERMERE

We never must be again. Oh Arthur, don't love me less,
and I will trust you more. I will trust you absolutely. Let
us go to Selby. In the Rose Garden at Selby the roses are   400
white and red. love + innocence.

Enter LORD AUGUSTUS *C.*

LORD AUGUSTUS

Arthur, she has explained·everything! (LADY WINDERMERE
looks horribly frightened at this. LORD WINDERMERE *starts.*
LORD AUGUSTUS *takes* WINDERMERE *by the arm and brings
him to front of stage. He talks rapidly and in a low voice.* LADY
WINDERMERE *stands watching them in terror*) My dear fellow, she has explained every demmed thing. We all
wronged her immensely. It was entirely for my sake she   405
went to Darlington's rooms. Called first at the Club—fact
is, wanted to put me out of suspense—and being told I had
gone on—followed—naturally frightened when she heard a
lot of us coming in—retired to another room—I assure you,
most gratifying to me, the whole thing. We all behaved   410
brutally to her. She is just the woman for me. Suits me
down to the ground. All the conditions she makes are that
we live entirely out of England. A very good thing, too.
Demmed clubs, demmed climate, demmed cooks,
demmed everything. Sick of it all!   415

LADY WINDERMERE (*Frightened*)

Has Mrs Erlynne—?

---

405 *wronged her immensely* after this sentence T, C1, and LC have: 'we are greatly
to blame'.

411 *brutally to her* after this sentence T and LC have: 'Egad! if anyone says
anything against her now, I'll call him out, my boy. I'm damned if I won't.
Even if it's a case of pistols for two and coffee for nobody afterwards'. C1 is
similar.

LORD AUGUSTUS (*Advancing towards her with a low bow*)
  Yes, Lady Windermere—Mrs Erlynne has done me the
  honour of accepting my hand.
LORD WINDERMERE
  Well, you are certainly marrying a <u>very clever woman</u>!
LADY WINDERMERE (*Taking her husband's hand*)
  Ah, you're marrying a <u>very good woman</u>! 420

Act-Drop

everyone is deceived
by Mrs. E.

Mrs. E. gets rewarded for her
actions.

418 *accepting my hand* after this speech C1 and T have:

> LADY WINDERMERE
>   Oh! I am so pleased!

APPENDIX

Two episodes have been selected from Act II to demonstrate the care with which Wilde undertook revisions. The first is the entry of Mrs Erlynne as it appears in C1, C2, and LC. The second is the end of Act II as it appears in C1, C2 and Cms, F, and T. The changes that occur in these passages are quite typical of the revisions that the play underwent as a whole. (Obvious errors of punctuation have been silently emended.)

The Entry of Mrs Erlynne (Evlynne)

C1 (A Good Woman: *Clark Library*)

BARKER
Lady Tedburgh and Lady Caroline Graham.

LADY JANSEN
Now wasn't that a most curious coincidence, Lord Windermere, and I haven't told you the most interesting part yet. The clergyman turned out to be the rector of our own parish, or the son of the rector, I forget which.

BARKER
Mrs Evlynne.

LORD WINDERMERE *starts.* MRS EVLYNNE *enters very beautifully dressed and very dignified.* LADY WINDERMERE *clutches her fan. Then lets it drop on the floor. She bows coldly to* MRS EVLYNNE, *who bows to her sweetly and sails into the room*

LORD DAR
You have dropped your fan, Lady Windermere. (*Picks it up and hands it to her*) But how pale you are.

LADY WIN
Cowards are always pale.

MRS EVLYNNE
How do you do, Lord Windermere? How charming . . . your wife looks to-night? Quite a picture.

LORD WIN (*In a low voice*)
How rash of you to come.

MRS EVLYNNE (*Smiling*)
Oh! No, it was the wisest thing I ever did in my life. And

by the way you must pay me a good deal of attention to-night. I know scarcely anyone here, and I am afraid of the women. You must introduce me to some of them. The men I can manage.

BARKER

Sir James and Lady Royston.

LORD WIN

You don't know what has happened. Someone has told my wife. . . .

MRS EVLYNNE

What? Not everything? No one knows.

LORD WIN

Not everything, I am glad to say, but my wife has seen my bank book with all. . . .

MRS EVLYNNE

Yes; yes. That is rather annoying, well, what did you say? Didn't you tell her you were my trustee, or something of that kind.

LORD WIN

No, it never occurred to me.

BARKER

Mr & Mrs Arthur Rowley, Lady Lennox.

MRS EVLYNNE

Men have no brains. I have got out of fifty scrapes worse than that.

BARKER

Lord & Lady Plymdale. Sir Hector Erskine.

LORD WIN

You don't know what I have been going through.

MRS EVLYNNE (*Shrugging her shoulders*)

My dear boy, I am very sorry for you, but my coming here was absolutely necessary. I don't think I'll trouble you much again. Tonight is my night of victory, a very critical night. After this I shall be able to take care of myself.

BARKER

Sir George and Lady B. The Misses B.

MRS EVLYNNE

That is Lord Augustus, isn't it?

LORD WIN

Yes, is he going to propose?

MRS EVLYNNE

No, but I am. How do you do Lord Augustus. You have quite neglacted [*sic*] me lately. I have not seen you since yesterday.

LORD AUG

My dear Mrs Evlynne . . . I assure you . . .

MRS EV

No. I see you're faithless. Every-one told me so.

LORD AUG

Now really . . .

LORD DAR

You look faint, Lady Windermere. Come out on the ter-race. The air is lovely there.

LADY WIN

Yes; I will come out. Barker send my cloak out to the terrace.

C2 (Lady Windermere's Fan: *Clark Library)*[1]

LORD W (*Standing R.C.*)

I must tell her the truth. If anything were to happen here, it would be terrible.

LADY W

I want a friend to-night, Lord Darlington. I didn't know I would want one so soon.

LORD D

Lady Windermere, I knew the time would come some day; but why to-night?

LORD W

I'll tell her now.

PARKER

Mrs Erlynne!

LORD WINDERMERE *starts.* MRS ERLYNNE *enters L. very beauti-fully dressed and very dignified.* LADY W *clutches at her fan, then lets it drop on the floor. She bows coldly to* MRS E, *who bows to her sweetly, and sails into the room*

MRS E (*Crossing C.*)

How do you do, Lord Windermere?

LORD AUGUSTUS *enters R.* LORD D *picks up fan and hands it to* LADY W

MRS E (*C.*)

How charming Margaret looks to-night. Quite a picture!

LORD W (*C. in a low voice*)

It was terribly rash of you to come!

---

[1] The s.d. in the two C2 typescripts differ slightly.

MRS E (*Smiling*)

It was the wisest thing I ever did in my life. And, by the way, you must pay me a good deal of attention this evening. I am afraid of the women. You must introduce me to some of them. The men I can always manage. (LORD W *goes up and watches* MRS E) (*To* LORD A *who is* R.) How do you do, Lord Augustus? You have quite neglected me lately. I have not seen you since yesterday. I am afraid you're faithless. Everyone told me so.

LORD A (*R.*)

Now really, Mrs Erlynne, let me explain!

MRS E (*R.C.*)

No, dear Lord Augustus, you can't explain anything. It is your chief charm.

LORD A

Ah! if you find charms in me, Mrs Erlynne—

LORD D

How pale you are.

LADY W

Cowards are always pale.

MR B *enters with* JEDBURG

LORD D

Come out on the terrace.

LADY W

Yes. (*To* PARKER *who is standing* L.) Parker, send my cloak out.

LC (*Licensing Copy of* Lady Windermere's Fan: *British Library*)

LADY W (*C.*)

. . . I want a friend to-night, Lord Darlington. I didn't know I would want one so early.

LORD [D]

Lady Windermere, I knew the time would come someday: but why to-night?

PARKER

Mrs Erlynne.

LORD WINDERMERE *starts.* MRS ERLYNNE *enters L., very beautifully dressed and very dignified.* LADY W *clutches at her fan, then lets it drop on the floor. She bows coldly to* MRS E, *who bows to her sweetly, and sails into the room*

MRS E (*Crossing C.*)

 How do you do, Lord Windermere?

LORD D

 You have dropped your fan, Lady Windermere. (*Picks it up and hands it to her*) But how pale you are!

LADY W

 Cowards are always pale!

MRS E (*C.*)

 How charming your wife looks to-night. Quite a picture!

LORD W (*C. in a low voice*)

 It was terribly rash of you to come.

MRS E (*Smiling*)

 It was the wisest thing I ever did in my life. And by the way, you must pay me a good deal of attention this evening. I am afraid of the women. You must introduce me to some of them. The men I can always manage. (*To* LORD A *who is* R. LORD W *goes up and watches* MRS E) How do you do, Lord Augustus? You have quite neglected me lately. I have not seen you since yesterday. I am afraid you're faithless. Every one told me so.

LORD A (*R.*)

 Now really, Mrs Erlynne, let me explain.

MRS E (*R.C.*)

 No, dear Lord Augustus, you can't explain anything. It is your chief charm.

LORD A

 Ah, if you find charms in me, Mrs Erlynne—

Goes to LADY J, *R. corner*

LORD D

 You look faint, Lady Windermere. I understand everything now. Shall we go on the terrace?

LADY W

 Yes, I'll come. (*To* PARKER, *who is standing L.*) Parker, send my cloak out.

The End of Act II

C1 (A Good Woman: *Clark Library*)

MRS EV

 A letter addressed to her husband! (*Takes up letter*) . . . No, no. It would be impossible. Life doesn't repeat its tragedies, like that. I must see what is in it. I must. (*Opens letter*) Oh! (*Sinks into a chair*) How terrible. The same letter that twenty years ago I wrote to my husband, and how bitterly I have been punished for it . . . No. My punishment, my real punishment, is tonight, is now. What shall I do. How terrible! How terrible.

Enter LORD WINDERMERE

LORD WIN
Have you bid good-night to my wife?
MRS EV (*Crushing letter in her hand*)
Yes.
LORD WIN
Where is she?
MRS EV
Oh! she is very tired. She has gone to bed. She said she had a slight headache, and . . . didn't wish to be disturbed.
LORD WIN
I must go to her.
MRS EV
Oh, no. Its [*sic*] nothing, nothing serious. She's only tired, that is all. Besides, there are heaps of people still in the supper room. She wants you to make her excuses to them. (*Drops letter*) She asked me to tell you.
LORD WIN
You have dropped something.   *Picks up letter*
MRS EV
Oh! yes. Thank you, that is mine.   *Takes letter*
LORD WIN
But its [*sic*] my wife's handwriting, isn't it?
MRS EV
Yes, its [*sic*] . . . something I asked her to write down for me . . . an address.
LORD WIN
She was charming to you?
MRS EV
Quite charming.
LORD WIN
You're faint.
MRS EV
No: its [*sic*] nothing. Will you ask them to call my carriage please.
LORD WIN
Certainly.

MRS EV

Thanks. (*Exit* LORD WINDERMERE) What can I do? I must get Windermere out of the house somehow, or he will discover everything.

Enter LORD AUGUSTUS

LORD AUG

Dear Lady, I have been looking all over the place, for you. May I not have the honour of seeing you home.

MRS EV

Lord Augustus, listen to me. You are to take Lord Windermere down to your Club to-night, at once, and keep him there as long as possible. You understand.

LORD AUG

But I don't understand. Why should I take Windermere?

MRS EV

Oh! don't ask why. Do what I tell you.

LORD AUG

And my reward?

BARKER

Mrs Evlynne's carriage is waiting.

MRS EV

Oh! You bother me. But don't let Windermere out of your sight. If you do I shall never forgive you.   *Exit*

LORD AUG

Well, really upon my word . . . this is dammed extraordinary.

C2 and Cms (Lady Windermere's Fan: *Clark Library*)[2]

MRS E

Gone out of her house! A letter addressed to her husband! (*Takes up letter*) No, no! It would be impossible! Life doesn't repeat its tragedies like that! Oh why does this horrible fancy come across me? Why do I remember now the one moment of my life I most wish to forget? *Does* life repeat its tragedies? I must see what is in it, I must. (*Goes to table and opens letter*) Oh! (*Sinks into a chair*) How terrible! The same words that twenty years ago I wrote to her father, and how bitterly I have been punished for it!

---

[2] There are very slight differences in the punctuation and the s.d. in these drafts. The text given is the second typescript in C2.

No, my punishment, my real punishment is to-night, is
now! *Still seated R.*

(*Enter* LORD WINDERMERE *L.U.E.*)

LORD W

Have you said good-night to my wife? *Comes C.*

MRS E (*Crushing letter in her hand*)

Yes.

LORD W

Where is she?

MRS E

Oh! she is very tired. She has gone to bed. She said she had
a headache.

LORD W

I must go to her. (*Moves L.C.*) You'll excuse me?

MRS E (*Rising and going R.C.*)

Oh no! It's nothing serious. She's only very tired, that is
all. Besides, there are people still in the supper room. She
wants you to make her apologies to them. She said she
didn't wish to be disturbed. (*Drops letter*) She asked me to
tell you!

LORD W (*Picks up letter*)

You have dropped something.

MRS E

Oh yes. Thank you, this is mine. *Takes it*

LORD W

But it's my wife's handwriting, isn't it?

MRS E

Yes, it's an address. Will you ask them to call my carriage
please?

LORD W

Certainly. *Goes L. and exits*

MRS E

Thanks! What can I do? What can I do? I feel a passion
awaking within me that I never felt before. What can it
mean? The daughter must not be like the mother—that
would be terrible. How can I save her? A moment may
ruin a life. Who knows that better than I? Windermere
must be got out of the house—(*Enter* LORD AUGUSTUS,

R.U.E., carrying bouquet) that is absolutely necessary.
(*Goes L.*) But how shall I do it? It must be done somehow.
Goes R.

LORD A

Dear lady, I am in such suspense! I haven't had a single
dance with you.

MRS E

Lord Augustus, listen to me. You are to take Lord Windermere down to your Club to-night, at once. Keep him
there as long as possible. You understand?

LORD A (*R.C.*)

But I don't understand.

MRS E (*Crossing L.C.*)

Do what I tell you. Keep him at your club. Keep him there
for hours. Don't let him out of your sight. If you do I'll
never forgive you. I'll never speak to you again. Remember
you're to keep Windermere at your club. And don't let him
come back to this house to-night!   *Exit L.*

F (Lady Windermere's Fan: *French's Acting Edition*)

MRS E

Gone out of the house! A letter addressed to her husband!
(*Takes up letter*) No, no! It would be impossible. (*Sits*)
Life doesn't repeat its tragedies like that. Oh! why does
this horrible fancy come across me? Why do I remember
now the one moment of my life I most wish to forget? *Does*
life repeat its tragedies? (*Opens letter*) Oh, how terrible!
(*Sinks into a chair*) The same words that twenty years ago I
wrote to her father; and how bitterly I have been punished
for it! No; my punishment is to-night—is now!
Still seated R.

Enter LORD WINDERMERE *L.U.E.*

LORD W (*Coming C.*)

Have you said 'Good-night' to my wife?

MRS E (*Crushing letter in her hand*)

Yes.   *Hides letter under her fan*

LORD W

Where is she?

MRS E

Oh, she is very tired. She has gone to bed. She said she had a headache.

LORD W

I must go to her. (*Moves L.C.*) You'll excuse me?

MRS E (*Rising and going R.C.*)

Oh, no! It's nothing serious. She's only very tired, that is all. Besides, there are people still in the supper room. She wants you to make her apologies to them. She said she didn't wish to be disturbed. (*Drops letter*) She asked me to tell you.

LORD W (*Picks up letter*)

But you have dropped something.

MRS E

Oh, yes, thank you; that is mine.   *Takes it*

LORD W

But it's my wife's handwriting, isn't it?

MRS E

Yes; it's—an address. Will you ask them to call my carriage, please?

LORD W

Certainly.   *Goes L. and exit*

MRS E

What can I do? What can I do? I feel a passion awakening within me that I never felt before. What can it mean? The daughter must not be like the mother—that would be terrible. How can I save her? A moment may ruin a life. Who knows that better than I? Windermere must be got out of the house, that is absolutely necessary. (*Goes up*) But how shall I do it? It must be done somehow.   *Goes R.*

Enter LORD AUGUSTUS *R.U.E., carrying bouquet*

LORD L[ORTON]

Dear lady, I am in such suspense! I haven't had a single dance with you.   *L.C.*

MRS E (*R.C.*)

Lord Augustus, listen to me. You are to take Lord Windermere down to your club to-night, at once. Keep him there as long as possible.

LORD L[ORTON] (*C.*)

But you said you wished me to keep early hours!

MRS E

Do what I tell you!

LORD L[ORTON]

And my reward?

MRS E

Oh! ask me that to-morrow, but don't let Windermere out of your sight to-night. If you do I will never forgive you. I will never speak to you again. I'll have nothing to do with you. Remember, you are to keep Windermere at your club. And don't let him come back to-night.

Exit C.; LORD AUGUSTUS *rushes after her, meets* PARKER *in door, drops flowers and exits*; PARKER *picks them up and goes off*

T (A Good Woman: *University of Texas*)
(the ms revisions to this draft are not noted)

MRS E

Gone out of her house! A letter addressed to her husband! (*Takes up letter*) No, no! It would be impossible. (*Sits*) Life doesn't repeat its tragedies like that. I must see what is in it. I must! (*Opens letter*) Oh! (*Sinks into a chair*) How terrible! The same letter that twenty years ago I wrote to my husband, and how bitterly I have been punished for it! No; my punishment, my real punishment is to-night, is now! *Still seated*

Enter LORD WINDERMERE, *L.*

LORD W

Have you bid good-night to my wife?

MRS E (*Crushing letter in her hand*)

Yes.

LORD W

Where is she?

MRS E

Oh! she is very tired. She has gone to bed. She said she had a headache, and didn't wish to be disturbed.

LORD W

I must go to her. You'll excuse me?

MRS E

Oh no! It's nothing serious. She's only very tired, that is all. Besides, there are people still in the supper room. She wants you to make her apologies to them. (*Drops letter*) She asked me to tell you.

LORD W

You have dropped something.   *Picks up letter*

MRS E

Oh yes, thank you, that is mine.

LORD W

But it's my wife's handwriting, isn't it?

MRS E

Yes; it's—an address. (*Takes letter*) Will you ask them to call my carriage, please?

LORD W

Certainly!

MRS E

Thanks! (*Exit* LORD W: *L.*) What can I do? What can I do? I must get Windermere out of the house somehow, or he will discover everything.

Enter LORD AUGUSTUS *R.U.E.*

LORD A

Dear lady, I have been looking all over the place for you. May I not have the honour of seeing you home? I am in such suspense!

MRS E

Lord Augustus, listen to me. You are to take Lord Windermere down to your Club to-night, at once, and keep him there as long as possible. Keep him there till morning, if you can. You understand?

LORD A

But I don't understand. You said you wished me to keep early hours!

MRS E

Oh, don't bother me! (*Crossing L.C.*) Do what I tell you.

Enter PARKER *L.*

PARKER

Mrs Erlynne's carriage.   *Exits L.*

LORD A

And my reward?

MRS E

Your reward! Oh! ask me that to-morrow, but don't let Windermere out of your sight to-night. If you do, I shall never forgive you. *Exit*

LORD A

Well, really, upon my word—I suppose this should be damned gratifying to me; I am not sure that it is.